BACKYARD
LIVING

Designing & Planting
Backyards

KATHY SHELDON

TIME
LIFE
BOOKS

Contents

Introduction

What does the word *backyard* mean to you? That space you're forced to traverse when you take out the trash? The uninspired view from your kitchen window? The boring stretch of land between your back porch and your neighbor's garage? Pretend for just a moment that *backyard* can have a different meaning and mood. Imagine opening your back door early one summer morning and stepping into a place so enticing that you suddenly wonder why you bother to live indoors.

No matter what your imaginary backyard offers—terraced beds of flowers in full bloom or a hammock swaying in the dappled shade of a tree, a small waterfall's soothing trickle or the birds' melodic calls, the heady aroma of ripening apples or the clean scent of lavender—this backyard can be yours.

Start by browsing through the pages of this book. If you long for a quiet outdoor hideaway, protected from the sights and sounds of traffic, you'll probably find yourself lingering over the section on designing yards for privacy. If your children (and the neighbors' children and the family pets) are clamoring for safe space in which to play, head for the section on designing yards for families. Perhaps you're the sensual type, whose garden fantasies focus on aromatic and culinary delights; or a budding herbalist who's always been curious about medicinal plants. *Designing and Planting the Backyard* offers plenty of information on all these topics.

You'll find a wealth of inspirational design ideas in this book, whether your garden goals are practical or playful, sophisticated or down-to-earth. You'll also find hundreds of helpful gardening tips, and a series of useful projects: Plant a miniature apple orchard, build a trellis for shade, start a container water garden, or create a terrace by building a dry-stacked stone wall.

You don't have to be an expert gardener or a professional landscape architect to transform your backyard into a space that you love. You don't even need a lot of time or money. You'll need to make friends with a spade and a trowel, of course, and to nurture your yard in return for the nurture it offers you. But once you learn how to work in tandem with Mother Nature, you can accomplish almost anything—including the backyard of your dreams.

Visual Variety

A carpet of summer grass may be deeply satisfying to mow, but you won't find yourself spending much time on that carpet if grass is all your yard has to offer. Why? Because staring at a lawn, no matter how green or lush, is just plain boring. Variety is the spice of any garden, just as it is of life.

An appealing backyard is one that offers a wealth of visual delights, from the continuously changing colors of its blossoms and foliage to the heights of its plants and the contours of the land itself. This yard may include a swath of healthy green grass, and you'll certainly find bright-blooming annuals in it each summer. A truly inviting backyard, however, will offer a feast for the eyes—and will offer that feast year-round.

In this special yard, you'll find beds of perennials and bulbs, bursting with color from spring to autumn; leaves in hundreds of shades of green, gold, and brown; planted berms or terraced slopes; evergreen ground covers peeking from under a blanket of snow; and more. And lest you think that this special yard can't be yours, read on...

Annuals, Perennials, and Bulbs

In spite of their sometimes intimidating Latin names, most flowers are easy to grow. Give them the soil they need, the sun they want, and a deep drink now and then, and most blooms won't care what you call them. Becoming familiar with the three main categories of flowers, how-ever—annuals, perennials, and bulbs—will help you decide where to place your plants and how to nurture them.

ANNUALS

Think of annuals as the gerbils of flowers. Their job is to reproduce as prolifically as possible in the short time they're with us—usually one season. Luckily, in order to create the seeds from which they reproduce, annuals must first flower—hence, their popularity.

ANNUAL: **Morning glory**

Annuals are an inexpensive, season-long source of color and some-times of fragrance. The plants—many of which are easily started from seed—creep, climb, and cascade. Unlike most perennials and biennials, they flower within weeks of germination, and after blooming for weeks on end, many will even sow seed for the fol-lowing year. For quicker color, pur-chase and set out bedding plants, which are often available in inexpen-sive six packs.

While a true annual is a plant that completes its life cycle in one season, the term "annual" is often used to describe any plant that will flower for only one season in a given climate, including biennials, which sprout from seed, produce only leaves the first year, and then flower and die during the second year. The term is also used for tender perennials that are unable to survive a particular region's harsh winters. In fact, many plants that we call annuals are perennial in milder climates.

Because they don't live long, annuals put down only shallow roots. Most aren't finicky about soil conditions and need only the correct amount of sunlight and water. Since an annual's goal in life is to produce seed, deadheading (removing faded flowers) is usually necessary to keep the plants blooming.

PERENNIALS

Although perennials die back to the ground each year, most have roots that can survive freezing temperatures to produce new shoots each spring. All perennials live at least three years, and some outlive their owners. Unlike annuals, most perennials flower for only a few weeks at a time. A perennial bed will change continuously (and with luck and planning, will bloom continuously) throughout the growing season.

Because a perennial has a short bloom time and a long life, you must consider its shape, foliage, and texture before deciding where to place one in your garden. Also remember that if an annual is like a gerbil, a perennial is more like a puppy; leave plenty of room for growth!

Perennials, which most home gardeners start from plants rather than from seeds, are usually more expensive than annuals, but the only care they require is occasional division or pruning. Of course, pruning reaps cut flowers and division produces more plants, so in the long run perennials are also economical backyard companions.

BULBS

Bulbs might be considered the camels of flowers; they store both moisture and nutrients in their fleshy tissues. Crocuses, daffodils, and tulips are well loved as harbingers of spring, but some bulbs (lilies and allium, for example) can also brighten perennial beds in midsummer, and some (as in the case of fall-blooming crocus) add color to autumn gardens.

BULB: **Siberian iris**

Bulbs do offer some challenges. Gardeners in the North must overwinter dormant tender bulbs indoors or plant new ones each spring. Gardeners in the Deep South must refrigerate hardy bulbs (40°F to 50°F or 4°C to 10°C) for six to eight weeks in winter because these bulbs require a period of cold in order to bloom. What's more, a bulb's foliage must be left to wither and brown so the bulb can build up nutrients for the following spring. To disguise the withered leaves, plant bulbs in beds with perennials or annuals that will grow to hide them.

Bulbs (the term is used for corms, tubers, rhizomes, and true bulbs) provide an astonishing variety of plants, from towering six-foot-tall cannas to tiny two-inch crocuses. As an extra bonus, some bulbs—when provided with well-drained soil—will naturalize (multiply and spread), either by seed or natural division, to provide a stunning return for a small investment of money and labor.

PERENNIAL: **Shasta daisy**

An Annual, Perennial, and Bulb Plan

There's no need to segregate your flowers by type: This combination of annuals, perennials, and bulbs offers knock-your-socks-off color all summer long. The perennials in this garden will only get better with time, the summer-blooming bulbs require practically no care, and the annuals will flower with gusto all season. Because the low-growing annuals are at the front of the bed, they can be replaced easily each year.

A LADYBELLS
Adenophera confusa

Hardiness zones 3–8

36 inches tall

Spires of nodding, bell-shaped, deep blue flowers in summer; toothed leaves; rich, moist, well-drained soil; full sun to partial shade

B ROSE CAMPION
Lychnis coronaria

Hardiness zones 4–9

30 inches tall

Small, rounded, magenta flowers in summer; wooly, gray-green leaves; moist, well-drained soil; full sun to partial shade

C LILY
Lillium 'Mont Blanc'

Hardiness zones 3–8

30 inches tall

Large, unscented, bowl-shaped, white flowers, flecked with brown, bloom in summer; glossy, dark green leaves; moist, well-drained soil; full sun to light shade

D PETUNIA
Petunia 'Purple Wave'
and 'Lilac Wave'

Annual

up to 18 inches tall

Trumpet-shaped, 3- to 5-inch flowers all summer (*P.* 'Purple Wave' is magenta; *P.* 'Lilac Wave' is lavender); sticky, hairy green leaves; well-drained soil; full sun

E GOLDEN EYE
Bidens 'Golden Eye'

Annual

up to 12 inches tall

Small, daisy-like, golden yellow flowers all summer; finely cut, delicate leaves on wiry stems; moist, well-drained soil; full sun

F CANDYTUFT
Iberis

Hardiness zones 5–9

6 to 18 inches tall

Clusters of tiny white, pink, red, or violet flowers spring through summer; dark green leaves; well-drained soil; full sun

G TOADFLAX (BUTTER AND EGGS)
Linaria vulgaris

Hardiness zones 4–8

12 to 36 inches tall

Small, pale yellow and white flowers resembling snapdragons from late spring to autumn; pale green, linear leaves; light, well-drained (preferably sandy) soil; full sun

H SPEEDWELL
Veronica alpina 'Alba'

Hardiness zones 4–8

up to 16 inches tall

Long spikes of tiny white flowers spring to summer; soft-textured, narrow leaves; well-drained loam; full sun to light shade

I YARROW
Achillea millefolium

Hardiness zones 4–9

24 inches tall

Flat-topped clusters of white, yellow, pink, or red flowers in summer; green or gray-green fernlike foliage; well-drained, poor soil; full sun

Improving Your Lawn

A lush, green lawn ties land-scape elements together, provides play areas, and even increases a home's value. Beautiful lawns do take some work, but too much coddling (over-watering, mowing, and fertilizing) does more harm than good. The best lawn-care system is one that concentrates on improving the soil and root growth.

AERATING YOUR LAWN

The soil beneath many lawns suffers from compaction. The cure is *aeration*—removing plugs of turf and soil in order to allow water, oxygen, and help-ful microorganisms to enter the ground.

The size of your lawn will probably determine how you aerate your soil. A spading fork will work for small areas, while a gas-powered aerator (available at tool-rental stores) will remove plugs from large lawns. If you've never aerated your lawn, do so twice a year (once in the spring and once in the fall) for the first two years. After that, aerate once every year or two.

FERTILIZING YOUR LAWN

Test your soil every few years to deter-mine its fertilization needs. Then em-bark on a regular fertilizing program and add sulfur (to lower pH) or lime (to raise pH) only as needed.

Self-mulching lawn mowers help fertilize your lawn by spreading finely-cut clippings, which provide nitrogen-rich organic material as they decompose. Other natural fertilizers, such as compost and manure, con-tribute to soil health and help your grass tolerate drought and com-paction. Although synthetic fertilizers are less expensive than organic alterna-tives, they often leach out of the soil easily and do not offer long-term soil improvement.

Apply fertilizers right before peri-ods of active growth—not during mid-summer. (A well-maintained lawn should need fertilizing twice a year at most.) And remember that overfertiliz-ing will cause excessive leaf growth—increasing the need for mowing—and insufficient root growth.

WATERING YOUR LAWN

Your lawn's water needs will depend on the type of grass planted and on the weather. Light, frequent watering dis-courages strong root growth (when water and nutrients are always available nearby, the roots have no reason to extend farther). To promote good root growth, provide large amounts of water less frequently, watering until the soil is moist to a depth of six to twelve inches.

Keeping the blade of a gasoline-powered lawn mower sharp and allow-ing the grass to grow a little longer than usual will decrease your lawn's need for watering. (Reel mowers necessitate more frequent mowing; they don't function well in very tall grass.)

OVERSEEDING YOUR LAWN

Overseeding (sowing grass seed on an established lawn) can improve an unattractive lawn or provide a temporary cool-season grass to cover dormant, brown grass in mild climates. It's an easy way to take advantage of the new grasses that are bred to resist pests and diseases and to tolerate shade, drought, and traffic.

When selecting a seed mix for overseeding, consider your climate, the amount of sun or shade your lawn receives, how much time you have for mowing and other maintenance, and how you use your lawn. (Yards that double as soccer fields need grass that can take abuse.) Consult with your local Cooperative Extension Service regarding mixes suitable for your area.

Overseed lawns in the North just before active growth begins in the early spring or late summer. Lawns in areas with mild climates should be overseeded when nearly dormant in the fall.

WEEDING YOUR LAWN

The healthier the soil, the fewer weeds you'll have to battle. (Of course, developing an appreciation for dandelions can also reduce weeding tasks!) When weeding is necessary, either remove the entire root by hand or apply herbicides. (The latter are toxic, so follow the manufacturer's directions carefully.)

ODE TO THE REEL MOWER

It begins shortly after daybreak on Saturday morning in suburban neighborhoods everywhere: a distant, whining drone that slowly gathers strength until its earsplitting racket drives children indoors and dogs beneath couches. Up and down the street, gasoline-powered, rotary lawn mowers are chewing up and spitting out grass, while belching fumes and complaining loudly.

Consider the reel mower. Its spiraled blades whirl and snip the grass with a satisfying swish and click—the sound of a dozen busy barbers. You can hear birds singing while you push a reel mower; you can smell the juicy green scent of fresh-cut grass. You can even hold a conversation over the fence with your next-door neighbor, assuming the neighbor isn't riding high in the saddle of a lawn tractor and wearing ear protection.

A reel mower does cut a narrower swath than a gasoline or electric mower, and because it works best on grass that

isn't very long, you'll need to mow more frequently. But for people with relatively small yards, the reel mower offers "reel" advantages. While rotary mowers bruise and tear grass blades, reel mowers cut cleanly. And speaking of clean, one recent study showed that lawn tools in Southern California put forth more pollution in a single day than all the aircraft in the Los Angeles area. What's the point of having manicured grass if you can't breathe when you go outside to see it?

Low-tech reel mowers are also economical. Although their blades require professional sharpening every other year, reel mowers don't require oil changes or last-minute trips to the gas station. They don't have a lot of complicated parts, so repairs are seldom costly. You can buy an old reel mower at a yard sale or purchase a newer model, which will be lighter and easier to maneuver. Either way, you'll be doing your part to make the world a little quieter and cleaner.

Planting for Color

Remember how exciting it was to open a new box of crayons when you were a child? Remember when you did things just for the joy of doing them, before you'd decided that you were good at some things and not at others? Well, you don't need a degree in landscaping or fine arts to plant a beautiful, colorful backyard.

COLOR THEORY

Children soon discover that when the green crayon is missing, they can color in a frog by blending blue and yellow. In the same way, a little knowledge about color theory will help you make each plant contribute more effectively to the color scheme of your yard. This is true whether you're the kind of gardener who sketches out every last leaf onto draft paper before heading to the nursery, or the kind who pulls into the drive with a carload of plants, wondering how on earth you'll cram them all in.

Let's imagine that your house has a patio with a small, fenced yard around it. If you know that warmer colors (yellow, orange, and red) tend to make objects appear closer, while cooler colors (blue, green, and purple) make objects recede, you might plant blue bellflowers beside the back fence in order to make your yard appear larger. If you'd like one part of your yard to stand up and shout, and another section to offer a peaceful sanctuary, knowing how color combinations affect mood will come in handy. Colors directly across from each other on the color wheel—red and green, blue and orange, yellow and violet—are called complementary colors. Placing complementary-colored flowers next to each other tends to create an exciting, vibrant effect. Colors adjacent to one another on the color wheel harmonize and produce a more tranquil, relaxing atmosphere.

FOLIAGE COLORS

Of course, you'll also need to consider foliage when you're planting for color. The leaves of different plants can vary from deep purple to silver to lime green. Certain foliage combinations can be quite dramatic and usually last longer than flower combinations. (See page 18 for more on foliage.) Trees, shrubs, and ground covers that are evergreen, as well as berries and dried grasses, all lend color to the landscape in winter.

INFLUENCES ON COLOR

Consider, too, when designing with color, every element of your yard. The house, its trim and roof, and even paving materials will add their own colors to the final composition—a composition that will change continuously from hour to hour, week to week, and season to season. In mixed perennial beds, the color scheme will change almost weekly, so you must consider bloom time when planting. (No matter how perfect that pink peony might look next to a purple aster, you'll never see their flowers at the same time.) Pale evening primroses, lost in the glare of the afternoon sun, will practically glow in twilight. The light during different seasons of the year will also change the appearance of colors.

Luckily, nature helps out when it comes to coordinating seasonal colors. The bulbs and blossoms of early spring are often pastel; late summer flowers tend to be red, orange, and violet; while the fall palette is usually gold, rust, and purple.

All this information may seem like a lot to juggle, but if you trust your intuition and play around, you'll hit upon color combinations that will surprise and delight you. And if, as is almost inevitable, you also wind up with some hideous combinations, just grab your gardening spade and do what your third-grade art teacher always advised: "If at first you don't succeed . . ."

Toadflax (butter and eggs)

Glorious Green

Japanese painted fern

Are the shady sections of your yard forlorn and neglected? Does your garden look limp and exhausted in autumn and shamefully naked come winter? The antidote is to begin a love affair with leaves, and that means cultivating a passion for the various shades, hues, and tints of green.

The word *green* comes from the Old English word for "grow"; knowing this gives us a hint of green's importance to life. In fact, the green in plants comes from chlorophyll, which converts sunlight to energy through photosynthesis—a process upon which all life depends. Backyards with landscape designs that aren't working (yet!) often include too many plants selected for their flowers and too few for their foliage.

COLORS

From the reddish green leaves of a Japanese maple to the shocking chartreuse of a sweet potato vine, some shades of green can step forth from the backdrop of your yard to become outright show-stealers. Others—the silver, blue, and gray variations on green—can work to calm your color schemes and tone down hot spots. Do your fluorescent pink petunias clash with the red impatiens nearby? Tuck some silver dusty millers between them, and the effect will be magically harmonizing.

Then there are the plants that can't seem to make up their minds and put forth variegated foliage. These highly prized mutations, such as *Hosta* 'Royal Splendor', can light up a shady corner of your yard. The huge yellow-and-green striped leaves of the *Canna* 'Bengal Tiger' add an exotic, tropical touch to any landscape.

SHAPES

Foliage shapes vary widely. Think about the delicate fronds of a maidenhair fern; the huge, bold leaves of a rhubarb plant; and the stiff, swordlike leaves of an iris. When you group plants together, you should aim for both variety and repetition of foliage shapes. A garden bed filled with leaves that are too similar in shape will be boring. A bed cluttered with too many different leaf shapes will look busy. Once you begin noticing the shapes of leaves, you'll soon discover the fun of finding pleasing combinations. Teaming the lacy leaves of peonies with the upright blades of Siberian irises is a favorite foliage combination. Another is simple, heart-shaped hosta leaves planted beside the intricate foliage of ferns.

TEXTURES

Texture is as important as color and shape when it comes to designing with foliage. The leaves of some plants seem to beg for our touch. Two good examples are the feathery foliage of fennel and the woolly leaves that give lamb's-ears its name. Some leaves warn us to keep our distance—the shiny, sharply pointed leaves of holly and the spiny shields of thistle, for example.

In any landscape design, coarse-leaved plants come forward to meet the eye, while fine-textured plants recede. Setting a tree with fine-textured foliage (such as the honey locust or willow) toward the rear of your yard will make the yard appear larger, especially if you set a plant with bold-textured leaves (hostas work well) toward the front. Remember, though: Plants with large, coarse-textured leaves may overwhelm a very small space, just as fine-textured plants can get lost in large, open areas.

SEASONAL INTEREST

The fresh green of a perennial's new growth is always welcome in spring, but if you choose your perennials carefully, you can get autumn color from their leaves as well. Plumbago, cranesbill, and cushion spurge all have foliage that colors beautifully in the fall. Evergreens, of course, offer winter color, and also provide an ideal backdrop for spring and summer flowers.

Even if a love of flowers will always be what inspires you to grab the trowel and start planting, once you begin to see the potential of foliage in your landscape designs, you'll have both beautiful blossoms and a yard rich in visual variety all year long.

'Great Expectations' hosta

Lady's-mantle

10 Great Foliage Plants

- **'Blue Moon' hosta**
  Hosta 'Blue Moon'

- **Cushion spurge**
  Euphorbia polychroma

- **Dusty miller**
  Senecio cineraria

- **Gunnera**
  Gunnera

- **Japanese maple**
  Acer palmatum

- **Japanese painted fern**
  Athyrium niponicum

- **Lady's-mantle**
  Alchemilla mollis

- **Lamb's-ears**
  Stachys byzantina

- **Maidenhair fern**
  Adiantum

- **Plume poppy**
  Macleaya cordata

Conquering Slopes

First the bad news: Landscaping a steep slope can be frustrating. Even if you manage to coax grass to grow on it, mowing can be either treacherous or impossible. The soil on slopes is usually too dry for flower gardening. What's more, hard rains have a tendency to erode dry soil and leach out its nutrients.

Now the good news: Solutions for these problems exist. Some of the most beautiful gardens imaginable thrive on slopes that have been terraced or stabilized with rocks. The rise of a hillside shows many flowers to their best advantage, and rocks, which make handsome additions to almost any landscape, actually create a more moderate microclimate, which in turn will allow you to grow plants that might not otherwise survive in your zone. Attractive ground covers can serve to hold sloped soil in place as well. In addition, artificial streams and waterfalls look most natural when cascading down naturally sloping yards.

TERRACING

Terracing (creating a level section or sections) transforms a steep bank into usable land, fights erosion and nutrient loss by slowing and rechanneling water flow, and provides flat areas in which to plant or, if these areas are large enough, to dine or play.

Landscaping timbers, stones, and cinder blocks are all common materials for the walls with which terraces are constructed.

Whether or not you can create a terraced slope on your own will depend in part on the size and difficulty of the job, but anyone with a healthy back can create a low, dry-stacked terrace wall. (See page 24 for instructions.)

MAKING STEPS AND PATHS

Steps make a hillside garden more inviting and accessible, as well as easier to tend. The only firm rule to keep in mind as you build them is that they must be wide and deep enough to traverse easily. Many materials are suitable for making steps, including rocks, landscape timbers, and railroad ties. Some of the easiest steps to build—and the most convenient when you're dealing with large expanses—consist of gravel or wood chips spread within open frames constructed from landscape timbers.

Gentle slopes are often best served by meandering paths that cut back and forth across the slope rather than

steps that rise straight up the hillside. In fact, paths and steps that run across slopes are almost always your best bet for erosion control.

PLANTING GROUND COVERS

Many ground covers (see page 22) will quickly blanket a hillside and help curb erosion. Most require little maintenance, and the adverse conditions of the slope will cut down on the invasiveness of some ground covers. Evergreen ground covers, such as periwinkle, English ivy, and pachysandra, will give year-round coverage and may be interplanted with flowering bulbs. Low-growing shrubs, such as creeping juniper and cotoneaster, provide easy coverage for sloping terrain and are often able to thrive in spite of poor soil conditions.

WATERING SLOPES

Because water tends to run off sloping ground before it's absorbed, slopes should be watered at a slower rate than flat areas. Buried drip hoses positioned horizontally across a slope will allow water to weep slowly into the ground. Also keep in mind that because much of the water will run downhill, the top of a slope needs more water than the bottom.

Planting drought-tolerant flowers, shrubs, or ground covers on slopes will reduce the need to water. When you dig a hole for a plant on a slope, create a pocket by mounding the dirt just below the hole. Then, to hold the mounded dirt in place, bury a rock in its downhill side, tilting the top of the rock in toward the plant. The pocket will help hold water near the plant's roots until it is absorbed.

Using Ground Covers

Ground covers (low-growing, spreading plants) can add color and texture to shady areas, help control erosion on banks that are too steep to mow, and unite separate sections of the yard. Once established, ground covers both spread and thicken to become more attractive, usually with little if any maintenance.

CHOOSING A GROUND COVER

Before choosing a ground cover, consider the growing conditions of your particular site. Note the amount of sunlight the area receives and the condition of the soil. Some ground covers will grow in deep shade, while others need full sun. Some, such as vinca and ajuga, do well in dry spots, while others, such as sweet woodruff, will thrive in moist areas.

Think, too, about how you will use that section of yard and how you would like the ground cover to function. A creeping rose will blanket a slope with delicate color in summer. Pachysandra will provide year-round color and texture for your yard. Roman chamomile or thyme planted between paving stones will spread to provide a fragrant pathway to your

Cotoneaster

front door. (See page 46 for instructions on planting aromatic paths.)

Low-growing evergreen shrubs planted as ground covers can also add a vertical element to your landscape and will serve as visual transitions between grass or flowers and trees or tall fences.

PLANTING GROUND COVERS

Prepare the soil for ground covers as you would for any plant. If you're planting a large, flat area, rototilling

may be best. On a steep bank, you'll need to dig individual holes for each plant instead. Test the soil and amend it if necessary; then set out the plants, spacing them as directed. The most economical way to start fast-growing ground covers is to put in a few plants and be patient. To ensure even coverage on a slope, start at the top and stagger rows of the individual plants down and across.

Keep plants mulched and well watered until they're established. Vigilant weeding for the first year or two will reward you with a ground cover that needs very little weeding or other maintenance thereafter.

CONTROLLING INVASIVE GROUND COVERS

Some ground covers spread very rapidly and are planted for precisely this reason. These same ground covers, however, can get out of hand. When you come across catalog descriptions such as "extremely vigorous," or "covers that problem spot," watch out. Invasive ground covers can overtake an entire bed and threaten to swallow the house! Always plant these ground covers (English ivy, crown vetch, and ribbon grass are a few examples) alone and in areas bordered by hardscapes (cement pathways and stone terraces, for instance); solid barriers will keep the plants in check. Leaving a four-inch-deep, four- to five-inch-wide border of soil around the ground cover will also help control spreading. But even barriers won't prevent the need for regular pruning of underground stems and aboveground shoots at the edge of a vigorous ground cover's bed.

Ground Covers

COMMON & BOTANICAL NAME	HARDINESS ZONES	SOIL & LIGHT CONDITIONS	DESCRIPTION
African daisy *Osteospermum*	9–10	*well-drained* FULL SUN	tender perennial; purple to lavender to white daisy-like flowers; oblong leaves; blooms heavily in late winter and early spring; spreads to create a dense mat
Bugleweed *Ajuga*	3–9	*well-drained, acid loam* FULL SUN TO PARTIAL SHADE	perennial, but often evergreen in mild winters; whorled, violet, blue, pink, or white flowers in summer; thick mats of foliage in shades of green, deep purple, bronze, or creamy mottled white
Cotoneaster *Cotoneaster dammeri* 'Coral Beauty'	6–8	*well-drained* FULL SUN	prostrate, evergreen shrub; white flowers in summer; coral-red berries in fall; rich green foliage tinged purple in fall; fast growing
Creeping juniper *Juniperus horizontalis*	2–9	*light, well-drained* FULL SUN	evergreen, creeping shrub; scalelike foliage ranging in color from dark green to emerald to silvery blue-green, usually purple-bronzed in winter
English ivy *Hedera helix*	5–10	*average to poor, moist, well-drained* PARTIAL SHADE	evergreen trailing perennial; foliage ranges from butter yellow to dark green to purple, sometimes variegated; tolerates many conditions; can also be used as a climber
Pachysandra *Pachysandra*	5–9	*moist, well-drained, acid* PARTIAL TO FULL SHADE	evergreen or semi-evergreen perennial; short spikes with white or pink flowers in spring; whorls of toothed, dark green leaves; grows well beneath trees
Thyme *Thymus*	3–9	*average to poor, dry, well-drained, alkaline* FULL SUN	evergreen perennial or shrub; aromatic with rose-purple flowers in summer; tiny oval leaves; tolerant of heat and drought

Building a Low, Dry-Stacked Stone Wall

Dry-stacked stone walls require no mortar and are easier to create than you might think. Just be sure to complete only as much work in a day as your muscles can handle comfortably! The instructions that follow will work for any retaining wall two feet or less in height. If you like, you can adapt them to create either steps or terraced planting beds on a backyard slope. As you can see in the photo below, you may also taper a wall from one end to the other in order to match the incline of your yard.

MATERIALS & TOOLS

- Leather gloves
- Protective boots
- Shovel
- Mattock
- Stones
- ⅜" to ½" gravel
- Sturdy wheelbarrow for stones
- Sturdy 5-gallon bucket for gravel
- Steel rebar, 3' long

TIPS

- Calculate the amounts of gravel and stone you'll need by using the formulas below:

  Stone: (Wall length x wall height) + (wall length x wall width) = square feet of exposed wall. Divide square feet by 30 to calculate the number of tons of stone required.

  Gravel: (Wall height x wall length x 1 foot) ÷ 27 = cubic yards of gravel required

- Ideal stones are hard (basalt, gneiss, granite, and limestone are best) and have flat surfaces and well-defined corners. Order 35 percent more stone than required for your wall and select the best stones from the pile.

- Either order your stones from a stone yard or collect them from your property. Gravel is available from sand and gravel companies.

Instructions

1 Select some of the largest, flattest stones for the top layer of your wall and set these "capstones" aside. (Be sure to wear protective clothing, including leather gloves and boots.)

2 Using your mattock and shovel, cut away the soil bank, angling it slightly backward from bottom to top. (Save some of the soil; see step 10.)

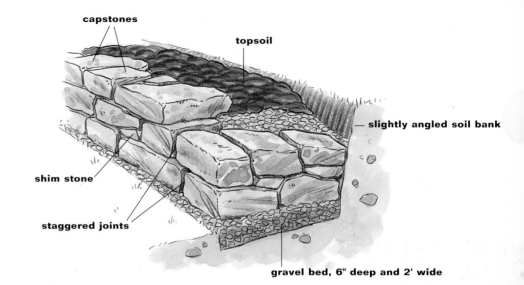

3 Dig a 6"-deep, 2'-wide trench at the base, and fill it with gravel. Then spread a 2"-thick layer of gravel from the base of the cut bank to the front of the trench.

4 Select very large stones, each with at least one wide, flat surface, for the first layer. Position their front ends as close to each other as possible, at the front of the trench, and their flattest surfaces facing up. (The distance between the soil bank and the back of each stone will vary, but should average about 1'.) Slant each stone slightly downward from front to back, and set any long, rectangular stones with their short ends positioned at the front and back of the layer.

5 To create corners at each end of your wall and to keep the gravel from filtering out, set stones to fill the gap between the soil bank and the first and last stones in this layer.

6 Add gravel behind the first layer of stones, filling the gaps between the back ends of the stones as well. To lock the stones in place and fill all the voids between them, "set" the gravel around their sides and backs by jabbing it repeatedly with one end of the rebar. (Add more gravel as necessary.) When you're finished, brush away any gravel on top of the stones. Backfilling a wall with gravel and setting the gravel can be tedious, but both steps are essential for wall strength and stability.

7 Lay out the next layer of stones. To make your wall stronger, stagger the joints between the stones in each layer by setting each stone on top of a joint in the layer beneath. Stabilize wobbling stones by using small rocks as shims. Use especially long stones as "ties" by setting them with one short end in front and the other short end right up against the soil bank in back.

8 Add gravel behind the stones in the second layer, and set the new gravel with the rebar.

9 Continue by adding layers of stone, backfilling with gravel, and setting the gravel after each layer is complete. As you work, check frequently to make sure that each layer is level from end to end and angled slightly downward from front to back. Also make sure the outer face of the wall angles slightly backward from bottom to top. The slope of the wall should match the slope of the cut soil bank.

10 Using the capstones that you set aside in step 1, lay out the last layer of your wall, and then backfill with gravel as before. Then cover the gravel with the soil you reserved in step 2.

Privacy &
Relaxation

Read this chapter with your feet up. For a few minutes, set aside thoughts of stacking stones, pulling weeds, and mowing grass. Stretch out on a chaise or curl up in a swing, and think relaxation.

Imagine yourself lounging in a hammock, late one summer afternoon. The breeze is playing in the leaves above; a waterfall spills into a small pond nearby. Or envision yourself sitting on a rustic bench in your own private garden nook, watching birds play at your garden fountain. Or perhaps you'd rather read while resting in the shade of trellised vines.

Every yard needs a private sanctuary—a place that offers respite from the rest of the world and promises peace of mind. And don't worry. A private place doesn't have to be ringed by high, ugly fences or gloomy hedges: Tall plantings that shelter and water features that soothe are more calming—and much more attractive. Let yourself be inspired, but don't grab that shovel yet! First, sit back and practice the fine art of relaxation.

Planting for Privacy and Relaxation

Imagine your house without any walls. How could you possibly relax and enjoy yourself, exposed to both your neighbors and the elements? Our backyards, like our homes, are places in which we need a sense of privacy and comfort. Unfortunately no one told that to the designers of many modern housing developments, where adjoining yards sometimes merge into one and are open on all sides.

Fences, trees, hedges, trellised vines, and even tall perennial plantings will define the boundaries or "walls" of your property to make you feel more secure and protected. Yards designed with careful attention to these vertical elements will put you and your guests at ease and encourage relaxation.

Tall plantings often serve more than one function at a time. As we scan seed catalogs in January, most of us crave sunlight, but on a July afternoon, lounging on an unsheltered patio may make you feel as relaxed as a hot dog on a grill. A strategically placed, vine-covered trellis can provide color and even fragrance while it casts cooling shade onto your patio.

Trees and shrubs that screen out the sights and sounds of traffic can also buffer a seaside home from strong winds. The fence that offers privacy from the neighbors can become the home for an espaliered apple tree.

Even if your property is already fenced or hedged, vertical elements within the yard itself can break the space into a series of "rooms" that will greatly enhance your enjoyment of the space. Small yards actually feel larger when divided into separate areas. They're also easier to use. A line of low shrubs may be just enough to separate the kids' play area from your prized perennial bed, and during the summer, a tall perennial planting can set off a dining area from the rest of the yard.

As with all aspects of backyard landscaping, you'll want to keep vertical elements properly scaled to their site. Make sure that vine won't turn into Jack's beanstalk, and never plant a tree impulsively. Consider carefully the mature height of the species and the specific variety of any tree you'd like to plant. Removing an established tree that has grown too large or was planted in the wrong place is difficult and often costly. The right tree in the right place, on the other hand, will do wonders for your yard and might easily be enjoyed by future generations.

RELAX!

Why toil in the backyard all season if you're not going to prop up your feet and reap the benefits? Why fuss and fret over that perfect lawn and then deny yourself the pleasure of sprawling out on its fresh, cool grasses? Pick a sprig of that mint you started from seed, drop it into a tall glass of iced tea, and review some relaxing basics.

Sleeping. A nice, wide hammock wins the prize for best outdoor napping spot—hands down. Strung between two trees or spread out in its own stand, a hammock in dappled shade is the perfect place to read or sleep. Or read and then sleep. Or intend to read but fall asleep instead.

Sunbathing. Tsk-tsk, you know better than to bask unprotected. A big, floppy hat will help guard your face and shoulders, but you'll still need sunscreen with an SPF of 15 or higher to survive the sun's dangerous rays. Slather it on, and keep a big pitcher of ice water nearby to avoid dehydration.

Reading. There's no easier way to lose yourself than to slip between the pages of a good book. Settle into your favorite garden nook and check out these authors' observations of the natural world:

Pilgrim at Tinker Creek, **Annie Dillard**
My Favorite Plant, **Jamaica Kincaid**
New and Selected Poems, **Mary Oliver**
Plant Dreaming Deep, **May Sarton**
Walden, **Henry David Thoreau**

Gathering with Friends. Whether you want to grill kabobs, raise the volleyball net, or just sit and talk, there's no better place to host guests than in your well-tended backyard.

Observing Wildlife. You didn't plant all of those butterfly bushes for nothing, did you? Take time to find a quiet spot where you can sit and watch with fascination as butterflies flutter by, mantises pray, and cocoons burst. Even the smallest patch of a garden is teeming with life.

A Privacy Plan

An intimate backyard nook for leisurely chats or quiet contemplation is often the most treasured spot in the yard. The tall plantings in the garden plan provided here offer privacy, shade (if you set out your tallest plants to block the late afternoon sun), and cheerful bursts of color that will continue through the end of summer and into the fall. Space perennials (and the tree mallow) at least 18 inches apart. Keep the holly hedge sheared to 18 inches in height or replace the annuals behind it with taller perennials after the first year.

A **JOE-PYE WEED**
Eupatorium maculatum
Hardiness zones 3–7
up to 7 feet tall
Large, flattened clusters of white to deep purple flowers from midsummer to early fall; oblong, medium-green leaves on purple-tinted stems; moist, well-drained loam; full sun to partial shade; attractive to bees and butterflies

B **TREE MALLOW**
Lavatera 'Barnsley'
Hardy annual
up to 6 feet tall
Funnel-shaped, white flowers with red centers in summer, flowers fade to soft pink; gray-green leaves on vigorous, shrub-like branches; well-drained soil; full sun; deadhead to promote flowering

C **PHLOX**
Phlox paniculata 'David'
Hardiness zones 4–8
40 inches tall
Fragrant, flat, panicle-like, white flowers from midsummer to early fall; thin, lance-shaped leaves on sturdy stems; moist, fertile loam; full sun to partial shade; deadhead to prolong flowering

D **PURPLE CONEFLOWER**
Echinacea purpurea
Hardiness zones 3–9
2 to 4 feet tall
Deep purple to rose to white, drooping petals, with dark brown conical centers, blooms midsummer to early fall; lance-shaped, dark green leaves; well-drained loam; full sun to light shade

E FLOWERING TOBACCO

Nicotiana alata
Nicki Series 'Nicki Red'

Hardy annual

16 to 18 inches tall

Fragrant red, tubular flowers from midsummer to fall; spoon-shaped to ovate leaves; fertile, moist, well-drained soil; full sun to partial shade; flowers are especially fragrant at night

F ZINNIA

Zinnia elegans
Ruffles Series 'Pink Ruffles'

Annual

24 inches tall

Pink, ruffled, fully double flowers in summer; lightly hairy, oval leaves; fertile, well-drained soil; full sun; deadhead to prolong flowering

G JAPANESE HOLLY

Ilex crenata 'Hoogendorn'

Hardiness zones 5–7

3 to 4 feet tall

Dwarf evergreen shrub with small, glossy, medium-green leaves; moist, well-drained loam; full sun to partial shade

H ZINNIA

Zinnia angustifolia 'Star White'

Annual

24 inches tall

White, daisy-like flowers, with golden yellow centers, bloom until frost; oblong leaves lightly covered with hairs; fertile, well-drained soil; full sun; deadhead to prolong flowering

Additional Plants

1 **Weeping willow** (*Salix babylonica*)
2 **Hollyhock** (*Alcea*)
3 **'China Doll' rose standard** (*Rosa* 'China Doll')
4 **Whirling butterflies** (*Gaura lindheimeri* 'Whirling Butterflies')
5 **Bearded iris** (*Iris*)
6 **Globe amaranth** (*Gomphrena globosa*)

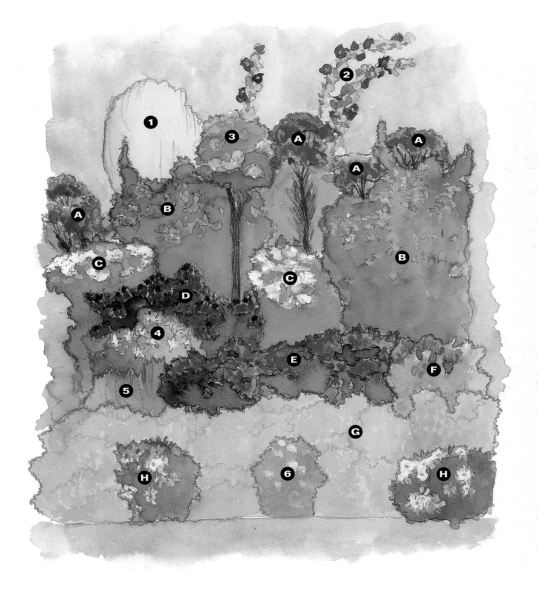

Building a Trellis Planter

This movable trellis provides privacy as well as shade from the hot summer sun—where you want it and when you want it. What's more, the unique, removable, double-planter design allows you to grow twice as many plants as you might on a typical trellis. Just position this trellis so that the planter with sun-loving plants receives at least four to six hours of full sun a day. Put shade plants on the other side, and they'll thrive in the shadows of the plants behind them. (Don't worry if plants such as the impatiens shown below get some morning sun; as the day passes, they'll soon be immersed in shade.)

MATERIALS & TOOLS

- Measuring tape
- Pencil
- Straightedge
- No. 6 decking screws: 1¼", 1⅝", and 2"
- Handsaw or circular saw
- No. 2 Phillips-head screwdriver
- Electric drill with ⅛" and ¾" bits
- Coarse sandpaper, or router with ¼" roundover bit
- Exterior paint, or stain and sealer
- Paintbrushes

TIPS

- The instructions for this project substitute standard lumber for the milled cedar with which the actual project was built. (Standard lumber is considerably less expensive.) For parts L, M, N, and O, use weather-resistant wood, as standard lumber will rot too quickly, and paints, stains, or sealers may contaminate the soil.
- Predrilling ⅛" pilot holes for the screws will make screw insertion much easier.

CUTTING LIST

CODE	DESCRIPTION	QTY.	MATERIAL
A	Frame sides	2	1 x 6 x 78"
B	Frame top	1	1 x 4 x 48"
C	Base sides	2	1 x 2 x 15"
D	Base front and back	2	1 x 4 x 46½"
E	Base divider	1	1 x 2 x 45"
F	Crosspieces	3	1 x 2 x 46½"
G	Vertical lattices	3	1 x 2" x 53"
H	Vertical lattices	4	1 x 2 x 35½"
I	Vertical lattices	4	1 x 2 x 25"
J	Horizontal lattice	1	1 x 2 x 34"
K	Horizontal lattices	2	1 x 2 x 17"
L	Planter bottoms	2	1 x 8 x 44½"
M	Planter fronts and backs	4	1 x 8 x 46"
N	Planter sides	4	1 x 8 x 5½"
O	Planter legs	6	1 x 2 x 6½"

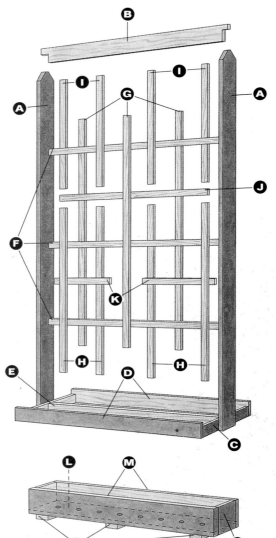

Instructions

1 Cut all the lumber to the lengths specified in the "Cutting List."

2 The top of each frame side (A) has two angled cuts. To mark these cutting lines, first measure and mark two points on the top edge of a frame side, 2¼" in from each long outer edge. Measure and mark two more points, one on each long edge, 2" down from the top end. Then mark lines between each pair of marks, and cut along the angled lines. Repeat with the other frame side.

3 At each short end of the frame top (B), measure, mark, and cut out a ¾" x 2½" notch.

4 Secure the frame top (B) to the angle-cut end of each frame side (A) by inserting a No. 6 x 2" decking screw through the outer face of each frame side (A), at a point 2" from its top end, into the vertical notched edge of frame top (B). Also insert a No. 6 x 2" screw down through the top edge of the frame top (B), into the top end of each frame side.

5 To make the trellis's base, first form a rectangle by arranging the base sides (C) between the base front and back pieces (D). Then secure each corner of the rectangle by inserting two No. 6 x 2" screws through the faces of the longer boards.

6 Center the base divider (E) within the rectangular base frame and fasten it in place by inserting two No. 6 x 2" screws through the outer face of each base side (C).

7 On a flat work surface, position the base between the frame sides (A), with all bottom edges flush and the frame sides centered on both ends

of the base. Then fasten the two assemblies together by inserting two No. 6 x 1⅝" screws through the outer face of each frame side.

8 Position one of the crosspieces (F) between the frame sides (A), centering it 40" up from the frame sides' bottom ends and across their widths. Attach this middle crosspiece by inserting two No. 6 x 2" screws through the outer face of each frame side.

9 Attach the remaining crosspieces (F) in the same fashion, centering one 20" up from the middle crosspiece and one 20" below it.

10 Position one vertical lattice (G) across the three crosspieces (F), centering it between the frame sides (A) and allowing it to extend 4½" below the lowest crosspiece. Fasten this lattice piece in place by inserting a No. 6 x 1¼" screw at each intersection. (Note: All the remaining lattice pieces are attached with No. 6 x 1¼" screws.)

11 Fasten the two remaining vertical lattice pieces (G), leaving 10" between the outer edge of each one and the inner face of each frame side (A).

12 Using the illustration and photo as guides, carefully position and attach all the remaining lattice pieces (H through K). Exact placement measurements aren't critical, but do be careful to attach the pieces to the correct side of the trellis frame.

13 To begin building each of the two planters, first attach the planter front and back pieces (M) to the two planter sides (N), using three No. 6 x 1⅝" screws at each corner.

14 Mark and drill a line of centered, ¾"-diameter drainage holes, spaced 5" apart, along the length of each planter bottom (L).

15 Place a planter bottom (L) inside each planter frame (M and N), and secure it with No. 6 x 1⅝" screws, spaced 6" apart and inserted through the faces of the planter frame boards.

16 Center the wide face of one planter leg (O) across a planter bottom (L), and fasten it in place with two No. 6 x 1¼" screws. Fasten two more legs across the planter bottom, positioning each one 3" in from an end. Repeat to attach the remaining three legs to the other planter bottom.

17 Using a router and roundover bit, or coarse sandpaper, round over all the edges of the planters and the frame.

18 Finish your completed trellis with exterior-grade paint or stain and sealer as desired. Don't, however, finish the planters' interiors.

10 Container Plants

for Shade

- **Dead nettle**
  Lamium

- **Fuchsia**
  Fuchsia

- **Impatiens**
  Impatiens walleriana

- **Wax begonia**
  Begonia

- **Wishbone flower**
  Torenia

for Sun

- **Dahlberg daisy**
  Dyssodia

- **Indian borage**
  Plectranthus

- **Narrowleaf zinnia**
  Zinnia angustifolia

- **Petunia**
  Petunia

- **Scented geranium**
  Pelargonium

Vines for Trellises

COMMON & BOTANICAL NAME	HARDINESS ZONES	SOIL & LIGHT CONDITIONS	DESCRIPTION
Black-eyed Susan vine *Thunbergia alata*	10–11	*Moist, well-drained, fertile* FULL SUN TO PARTIAL SHADE	3 to 6 feet; twining, tender perennial with small, trumpet-shaped flowers in shades of yellow, orange, and cream, usually with a dark center, blooms throughout the summer; triangular, mid-green leaves
Clematis *Clematis*	5–9	*Moist, well-drained, fertile* PARTIAL SHADE TO FULL SUN	4 to 30 feet; perennial climber with showy flowers in white, pink, or purple, spring to summer; leaf form varies greatly; prefers shade for roots but full sun for the rest of the vine
Honeysuckle *Lonicera*	4–11	*Moist, well-drained* PARTIAL SHADE TO FULL SUN	4 to 20 feet; perennial climber with small, fragrant yellow, white, pink, or red flowers spring to fall, depending on species; medium green foliage, some varieties evergreen or semi-evergreen; attracts bees and hummingbirds; can be invasive
Mandevilla *Mandevilla*	10–11	*Rich, moist, well-drained* PARTIAL SHADE	10 to 20 feet; tender perennial; woody, twining climber with pink or white, trumpet-shaped flowers in summer; often shiny, mid to dark green leaves; the flowers of some species are very fragrant
Morning glory *Ipomoea tricolor*	annual	*Well-drained, sandy* FULL SUN	15 to 20 feet; annual, twining climber with wide range of colorful, saucer-shaped, tubular flowers in summer; mid-green, heart-shaped leaves; *I. alba* (moonflower) has large, fragrant, white flowers that open at night
Passion-flower *Passiflora*	6–10	*Well-drained* FULL SUN TO PARTIAL SHADE	15 to 25 feet; tender perennial climber with multiple-colored flowers from spring to autumn, depending on species; usually three- to five-lobed, mid to dark green leaves; colorful, edible fruit; heavy growth requires sturdy support
'Jeanne Lajoie' rose *Rosa 'Jeanne Lajoie'*	5–10	*Rich, well-drained* FULL SUN	up to 8 feet; climbing miniature rose with lightly fragrant, two-toned pink blossoms borne in clusters from spring to fall; glossy, dark green leaves; must be trained to climb trellis
Sweet pea *Lathyrus odoratus*	annual	*Moist, well-drained* FULL SUN TO PARTIAL SHADE	6 inches to 6 feet; hardy annual bush or twining vine that bears fragrant, puffy flowers in a variety of colors in spring and summer; mid to dark green leaves; mulch to keep soil cool
Wisteria *Wisteria*	5–9	*Moist, well-drained* FULL SUN	up to 30 feet; perennial, woody, climbing twiner with white, pink or purple panicles of flowers in spring; bright green foliage provides dense shade; needs sturdy support; can be invasive

A Backyard Oasis

Water has an amazing range of effects. Gentle trickles and still pools of water soothe our spirits, while refreshing sprays invigorate them. Install a water garden, and you'll find yourself visiting every day to watch birds drinking at its edge, frogs singing in the rushes, and the aquatic ballet of water lilies unfolding on its surface. A few modern innovations make it easy to construct your own backyard oasis, even if your budget and available space are limited.

SELECTING A SITE

Before you decide what kind of pond you want, you'll need to choose a site. A water feature that you can see from indoors will provide more pleasure than one set away from the house, but if this kind of site isn't available, choose one close to a patio or low deck.

Water lilies and other aquatic plants require at least six hours of full sun each day. For pumps, fountains, and lighting features, the site should be close to outdoor electrical outlets. Avoid areas near trees, especially deciduous ones; they'll cast shade, send out marauding roots, and scatter falling leaves. Avoid low-lying areas, too; runoff may pollute your pond with pesticides and fertilizers. Finally, if children will be present in the area, either make your pond inaccessible to them or delay installing one until they're older.

WHAT KIND OF POND?

Most small backyard pools consist of either rigid fiberglass preformed shapes or flexible butyl liners. Preformed ponds are usually easiest to install, but liners allow you to determine a pool's shape and can be placed over large, smooth rocks, which you must excavate when installing a preformed pond.

Let the style of your house and yard help you select a design for your pond. Formal pools feature straight lines or geometrical shapes, while more natural-looking pools are curved and irregularly shaped. If you're installing a liner, use a hose to outline the size and shape of your pool. Before you start digging, view this imaginary pond from several perspectives and at various times of day.

The pond's size should be proportional to the landscape, but the larger

the pond, the less vulnerable it will be to pollution and temperature extremes. The water should be at least 18 inches deep, and—if you want to overwinter hardy fish—must include an area at least 24 inches deep.

Adding a waterfall to your pond is surprisingly easy. Waterfalls look best installed in naturally sloping areas. For flat sites, a few large rocks or boulders added to a mound of the excavated dirt can provide the slope for falling water. You'll need butyl lining for the waterfall portion, flat rocks and pebbles to hide the lining and provide the falls, and a pump to recycle and lift the water through a concealed pipe or tubing. Even if you don't include falls, your pond water may need a recirculating pump and filter to keep it healthy.

AQUATIC FLORA AND FAUNA

Most water gardens contain two types of plants: underwater ones (such as wild celery), which contribute oxygen, provide spawning nests for fish, and reduce algae growth by competing for nutrients; and floating ornamental plants, such as water lilies. Most floating plants prefer still water; situate them away from fountains and waterfalls. Many nurseries and home-improvement centers now stock a variety of water plants; ask for advice about which ones to choose, and beware of species that are invasive in certain parts of the country.

Birds, dragonflies, frogs, and snails will all be drawn to your water garden, but the sight of a bright orange fish darting beneath a lily pad is hard to resist. Fish also dine on mosquitos and other insects. (Before introducing fish to your pond, you'll need to treat the water with a chlorine neutralizer.) You'll find that these surprisingly attentive pets can become longtime companions. Goldfish can live for 10 to 15 years, and koi can live for decades.

Water Plants for Small Ponds

COMMON & BOTANICAL NAME	HARDINESS ZONES	DESCRIPTION
Chromatella water lily *Nymphaea 'Chromatella'*	3–11	hardy perennial; blooms abundantly over a long season, with canary-yellow petals surrounding deep yellow stamens; very fragrant; olive-green lily pads mottled in shades of chestnut-maroon
Pygmy water lily *Nymphaea tetragona*	4–11	hardy perennial (frost tolerant, but languishes in hot weather); 1½- to 2½-inch, white, star-shaped flowers; 3- to 4-inch lily pads
Siberian iris *Iris sibirica*	4–9	perennial; blooms from mid-spring to early summer, in deep blue, violet, white, or yellow; sword-shaped leaves; grows 2 to 3 feet tall; boggy iris for margins of small ponds
Tulip lotus *Nelumbo 'Shirokunshi'*	4–11	perennial; spectacular white, tulip-shaped, fragrant flowers on stems 18 to 24 inches tall; broad leaves, shaped like wide, shallow bowls, on separate 18- to 24-inch stems
Water hyacinth *Eichhornia crassipes*	8–11	potentially invasive perennial, controlled by state and federal laws; keeps water clear; showy violet-blue spikes, 4 to 9 inches tall; fine roots dangle from glossy green leaves
Water poppy *Hydrocleys nymphoides*	9–11	tender perennial; 2- to 2½-inch, lemon-yellow blossoms; slightly fragrant; small, oval green leaves; can overwinter in an aquarium in a sunny window

Water Elements on a Porch or Patio

Haven't got the room for even a small backyard pond? Not quite ready to take the splash into full-scale water gardening? Add a small water feature to your porch, deck, or patio, and you can still enjoy the enchanting effects of water.

You'll be amazed by all that water can do for even the smallest outdoor living space. Moving water weaves patterns as hypnotic as a flickering fire. Still water in a container garden will reflect blue sky and stars. Falling water, whether a trickle or a cascade, soothes as it blocks out distracting street noises.

CONTAINER WATER GARDENS

Container water gardens are the perfect feature for decks, patios, and porches. Almost any watertight, 10-gallon or larger container can become a miniature pond. For most aquatic plants, you'll also need a spot that receives at least four to six hours of sunlight a day. Half whiskey barrels and plastic liners for just this purpose are now available at many garden centers.

Along with water lilies, any number of handsome bog plants, floating ornamentals, and grasses are suited to container water gardens. Fish will help control mosquitos and other insects. Semitropical varieties such as gambusia (mosquito fish) and guppies can best survive the heat of a container garden in full sun.

MOVING WATER

Moving water will bring both music and motion to your outdoor living space. Features with moving water can be as elegant or rustic as your setting dictates. They can also vary in both size and complexity. Create a small raised pool with a waterfall on your patio or place a ready-made fountain in your porch corner or on a patio wall. Make your own whimsical table-top fountain from a small bowl, a submersible pump, plastic tubing, and the decorative material of your choice. (Many small fountains can even be moved indoors and enjoyed during the winter.) Just be sure to replace the water that evaporates from fountains, as the pumps will burn out if they're allowed to run dry.

Container Water Garden

Maybe you're not quite sure you want a water garden. At least, not sure enough to go out and start digging a large, deep hole in your yard. Why not get your feet wet with a small water garden in a container? This project uses a half whiskey barrel with a plastic liner (available at many gardening centers), but almost any clean, watertight container that will hold at least 10 gallons of water will do. The chart on page 37 lists other aquatic plants suitable for a container water garden.

MATERIALS

- Half whiskey barrel
- Rigid plastic barrel liner
- Water
- Chlorine neutralizer (optional)
- Clean rocks or bricks
- Aquatic plants (see list)
- One or two small semitropical fish (optional)

WATER DEPTHS FOR PLANTS SHOWN

- Parrot feather (*Myriophyllum aquaticum*), 3–12 inches
- Pickerel rush (*Pontederia cordata*), 1–12 inches
- Umbrella palm (*Cyperus alternifolius*), 1–6 inches
- Lizard's-tail (*Saururus cernuus*), 1–6 inches

Instructions

1 Rinse out both the barrel and the liner to remove any residue; then put the plastic liner inside the barrel. Position the barrel in the desired location, making sure it will receive at least six hours of sunlight a day. (The container will be very difficult to move once you've filled it with water.)

2 Fill the liner with water to within two to three inches of the liner's top. Let the water stand for two or three days; any chlorine in it must be allowed to evaporate. (Alternatively, add chlorine neutralizer as recommended by the manufacturer.)

3 Set your potted plants in the liner, using clean rocks or bricks to raise each plant so that its crown is submerged at the required water depth. (The list above gives the water depths for the plants shown in the photo.)

4 After 10 days (or at least one hour if you've treated the water with chlorine neutralizer) add one or two small semitropical fish, such as guppies or "mosquito fish" (gambusia), to help control mosquitos and other insects. (The water in container gardens can get too warm for cold-water fish such as goldfish or koi.)

5 Be sure to replace any water lost to evaporation. If you don't have fish you can add up to five percent of untreated new water at a time. If you do have fish, you'll need to use chlorine neutralizer each time new water is added.

Backyard Seating

For many of us in the workaday world, the outdoors is an area we experience when we trudge from the house to the car, or when we take out the trash. Sitting outdoors—actually remaining still long enough to let the natural world around you come into focus—is a particular pleasure, whether you're relaxing alone in a secluded garden nook or joining friends and family for an outdoor meal.

Outdoor seating—a swing beneath a rose-covered arbor or a wooden chaise beside a reflecting pool—becomes a part of the backyard architecture, what remains steadfast in a continually changing scene. A bench and a small table placed in just the right spot become more than a convenient place to relax; they create an instant tableau that's a part of your overall landscape design.

SELECTING SEATING

When selecting outdoor seating, consider both its form and its function. Attractive but uncomfortable chairs just won't be used. Delicate, whimsical furniture that's primarily garden decoration is fine, but seats intended for actual use should wear well and feel good when you're in them. Wood furniture should be well constructed from a rot-resistant or finished hardwood and should be properly joined—not glued. Hardware should be adequately sized and rustproof. Inspect all furniture before purchasing to make sure it's free of cracks or other flaws. (Crashing backwards onto the patio just as you're chomping into a ear of corn is definitely not relaxing!) Make sure, too, that your seating is sturdy enough not to topple over in high winds.

The color, material, style, and size of your outdoor furniture should complement rather than clash with your house and yard. An ornate, wrought-iron bench that looks stately in the formal gardens of a brick Colonial may look inappropriate in a bungalow's informal cottage garden. When it comes to color and style, remember that what seems trendy today may well appear dated a few years from now or may no longer be

appealing to you. Of course, if you paint wooden furniture, you can always change the color with little effort or expense, but the safest way to experiment with color and patterns is with pillows and cushions.

Gardening centers usually carry a variety of outdoor seats and benches, as do some department stores. Shops specializing in outdoor furniture will generally have the largest selection in a wide range of prices. Consider, too, mail-order catalogs, which sometimes offer build-it-yourself kits for everything from arbor seats to Adirondack chairs. Antique stores, junk shops, yard sales, and flea markets are all potential sources of unique or unconventional outdoor furniture. Never underestimate the power of a can of bright paint or a few cheerful throw pillows!

WHAT GOES WHERE

Once again, consider both the appearance and function of your seating when deciding where to place your outdoor furniture. A single lounge chair or bench tucked away in a private backyard corner is ideal for quiet relaxation. Hammocks are more enjoyable in shady spots, and if they catch the occasional breeze, so much the better. A bench at the end of a path provides a destination that encourages strolling; and seating backed by tall plants, shrubs, a fence, or a wall satisfies our very human need to feel protected and secure when we're relaxing.

Small backyard pools, evening gardens, and aromatic beds are all best appreciated from seat level. Place a bench or a few chairs beside any of these features, and your yard will become a place for leisurely watching fish swim and fireflies dance, instead of just a path to the trash can.

Building a Rustic Bench

A charming rustic bench offers a surprisingly comfortable place to enjoy the fruits of your labor and will look as if it grew right in your back-yard. Either cut fallen wood on your property, or make use of the tree branches that power companies, builders of new houses, and road construction crews often leave in their wake. (See "Tips" for special instructions.)

MATERIALS & TOOLS

- Tape measure
- Pencil
- Handsaw
- 4d and 16d galvanized nails
- Hammer
- Rope or twine (optional)
- Sandpaper

TIPS

- Try to use wood that is resistant to decay. Black locust, walnut, hornbeam, sassafras, cherry, cedar, and white oak all work well.
- Trees that have been felled in the fall and winter tend to hold their bark much better than trees cut in the spring or summer.
- Do avoid wood that's been lying on the ground too long; it's proba-bly already on its way to decom-posing and is best left to the bugs.
- For added stability, when you fasten any two pieces of wood together, hammer in each nail at an angle.

Instructions

1 Cut all the branches to the lengths specified in the "Cutting List." As long as the various parts are thick enough to be sturdy, exact diameters aren't important.

2 Lay two legs (A) flat on your work surface, 40" apart. Position one stretcher (B) across both legs, 2½" down from the top of each leg. Attach the stretcher to the legs with 16d nails. Repeat with the other stretcher and the other two legs.

CUTTING LIST

CODE	DESCRIPTION	QTY.	BRANCH DIAMETER X LENGTH
A	Legs	4	2¼" x 21"
B	Stretchers	2	2" x 48"
C	Long top end support	1	1½" x 25"
D	Long bottom end support	1	2" x 25"
E	Short top end support	1	1½" x 15"
F	Short bottom end support	1	2" x 15"
G	Bottom stringer	1	2" x 43"
H	Top stringer	1	1½" x 40"
I	Angle braces	4	¾" x 17"
J	Seat branches	27 (approx.)	½" to ¾" x 25"

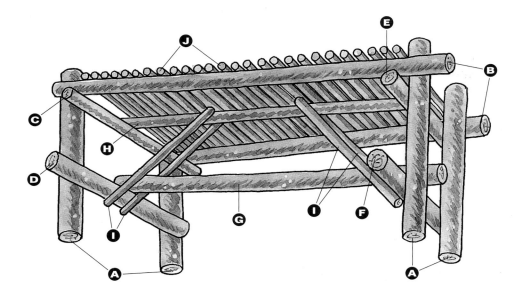

bottom end supports (D and F) and fasten it in place with 16d nails. Repeat to attach the top stringer (H) to the top end supports (C and E).

10 Position one angle brace (I) at a 40-degree angle so that it contacts one bottom end support, the bottom stringer, and the top stringer. Make sure the top of the angle brace doesn't rise above the top stringer, or the seat branches (J) won't rest flat on top of the stretchers (B).

11 Using rope to hold the angle brace (I) in place if necessary, attach it to the bottom end support and the bottom and top stringers with 4d nails. Repeat with the remaining three angle braces, turning the bench assembly as required.

12 At the widest end of the bench, use 4d nails to attach a seat branch (J) to both stretchers (B) and to the top stringer (H). Attach all the seat branches in the same manner, leaving ½" gaps between them.

13 Using the stretchers (B) as guides, cut the seat branches (H) so their ends are flush with the outer edges of the stretchers.

14 Lightly sand all cut branch ends if desired. This bench grows more beautiful as it weathers, so no protective treatment is necessary.

3 To begin assembling the wider end of the bench, first position one leg-and-stretcher assembly so that one leg (A) is flat on your work surface and the stretcher (B) and other attached leg stick up in the air. (To get the leg to rest flat on the work surface, you'll need to let the 2½"-length of protruding stretcher hang off the edge of the surface.)

4 Position the second leg-and-stretcher assembly similarly, 17" away from the first assembly and parallel to it. Have your friend hold the two stretchers upright for you.

5 Position the long top end support (C) in the interior corner formed by the legs (A) that rest on the work surface and the stretchers (B) that rise from them. Then fasten the long top end support to both the legs and the stretchers with 16d nails.

6 Place the long bottom end support (D) across the legs (A), 6" down from the long top end support (C). Attach it to the legs with 16d nails.

7 To assemble the narrower end of the bench, first turn the frame over carefully so the other two legs (A) are flat on your work surface, and both stretchers (B) extend upward. (Have your friend hold the frame in place again.) Pull the two legs on your work surface in toward each other until they're 6" apart. (Doing this will create the xylophone shape of the bench.)

8 Repeat steps 4 and 5 to fasten the short top end support (E) and the short bottom end support (F) to the legs (A) and stretchers (B).

9 Set the assembled bench frame on its feet. Center the bottom stringer (G) on top of and across the

Aromas & Flavors

A backyard should certainly offer visual delights and provide a sanctuary for quiet relaxation, but what about a yard that also yields a feast of fragrance and flavors? With just a little planning and care, your own backyard can become a private Eden of tantalizing herbs, edible flowers, and homegrown fruit.

Imagine the path from your back door carpeted with aromatic herbs spilling out from between paving stones. Imagine a yard brimming with scented flowers and herbs you'll harvest, dry, and share with friends while your garden sleeps beneath next winter's snow. Or perhaps you'll grow aromatics in a window box, so you can enjoy their fragrance or snip a sprig for dinner simply by opening a window. Plant edible flowers and turn even the simplest meals into something lovely. Start a miniature apple orchard, and in just a few years, you'll be enjoying homemade apple butter and golden-crusted apple pies.

You don't need a 10-acre homestead to realize these dreams. Even the smallest backyard can be lovingly coaxed and tended into a garden that awakens the senses with wonderful aromas and flavorful food.

Planting an Aromatic Pathway

A fieldstone or flagstone path or patio makes a striking design element for any backyard, but keeping the crevices between those stones weed free is time-consuming, back-breaking work. Cut weeding tasks to a minimum and create a fragrant carpet for your feet by planting hardy aromatic herbs between the pavers. The plants will soften the visual effect of the stone path or patio by tying it in with the rest of the landscape and will release their enticing aromas whenever you step on them. Most herbs can grow in dry, unfertile soil, and many varieties stand up to foot traffic remarkably well.

MATERIALS & TOOLS

- Asparagus fork or narrow trowel
- Hardy creeping herbs (see list)
- Water source
- Trowel or gardening spade
- Water-absorbing polymer crystals (available at gardening centers)
- Wheelbarrow or large bucket
- Topsoil
- Compost

TIPS

- Are the materials in your patio or path set too close to accommodate plants? Remove a few of the pavers and plant aromatics in the spaces left behind.
- The gravel bed beneath most stone paths and patios encourages moisture to drain from plant roots quickly, so water new plants deeply and frequently.

Instructions

1 Water all your plants while they're still in their pots. If you aren't planting in the early evening or on an overcast day, set potted plants in the shade until you're ready to transplant them.

2 Use a narrow trowel or asparagus fork to pull up all grass and weeds from between the stones. Make sure you remove the entire root of each weed.

3 Remove any gravel or sand from between the stones. Dig a hole slightly wider and deeper than the root system of the first plant you plan to put in.

4 Sprinkle a small amount of water-absorbing polymer crystals in the bottom of the hole. Mix the topsoil and compost together and add some of this mixture on top of the water-absorbing granules.

5 Set the plant into the hole, making sure its roots are able to spread out without bending or breaking.

6 Add more of the soil-compost mix to fill in around the plant. Press the soil gently to eliminate any air pockets.

7 Repeat steps 2 through 6 until the entire area is planted; leave at least 8 to 12 inches between each plant.

8 Water thoroughly and mulch with a 1"-thick layer of straw, pine needles, or shredded leaves. (The mulch may be removed after the plants are established.)

9 Water new plants frequently and avoid heavy foot traffic until the plants are well established.

10 Aromatic Herbs to Plant Between Pavings

- **Calamint**
  Acinos

- **Chamomile**
  Chamaemelum noblis 'Treneague'

- **Corsican mint**
  Mentha requienii

- **Miniature thrift**
  Armeria juniperifolia

- **Mother-of-thyme**
  Thymus serpyllum

- **Pennyroyal**
  Mentha pulegium

- **Pink chintz**
  Thymus serpyllum 'Pink Chintz'

- **Rock cress**
  Arabis blepharophylla

- **Woolly thyme**
  Thymus pseudolanuginosus

- **Winter savory**
  Satureja montana

Harvesting and Drying Aromatics

D on't spend the winter months pining for the aromas of summer. Capture the essence of your garden with a holiday potpourri made from the fragrant lavender or roses you tended so lovingly back in June. Many fragrant plants retain their scents well after drying. Some of the more popular categories of scents include citrus (lemon verbena), spicy (star anise), floral (scented geranium), and fresh (lavender).

Winters are also easier to bear with a pantry stocked with culinary and medicinal herbs. Imagine, for example, sipping a hot, hearty sage-flavored soup as snow blankets your summer herb garden. The tradition of drying herbs is thousands of years old and expresses our inseparable connection to the plant world.

HARVESTING

Gathering aromatics should be a relaxing, sensory pleasure rather than a chore. Let the fragrance of the sun-warmed plants wash over you; abandon gardening gloves (except, perhaps, for roses) and let aromatic oils scent your hands as you work. The best time of day to collect plants is on a sunny morning after the dew has dried and the sun has heated the plant's volatile oils. Picking plants when they're still wet encourages mold to grow on them, so go ahead and have that extra cup of tea instead. Try to avoid harvesting in the hot afternoon sun, as flower blooms will wilt.

Select plants that are free of insect damage, disease, and discoloration. Pass up plants exposed to pesticides, especially herbs that you intend to use for culinary purposes. If you'll be gathering plants beyond your yard and out in the wild, collect only a small number of any particular plant. Educate yourself as to which plants in your area are poisonous or endangered—leave these untouched—and remember that plants growing along roadsides may be contaminated with toxins.

To collect plants, you'll need pruning shears and a basket. Pruning shears cut plant stems cleanly, and help prevent the bruising and twisting that occur when stems are broken by hand. The basket allows plants to rest loosely in an upright position, so that blooms and leaves aren't crushed by the weight of other plants. It also allows air to circulate among the stems.

When harvesting flowers, cut the stems extra long, as some plants shrink to half their original size by the time they've dried. Most herbs will be at the peak of their flavor if they're gathered just before they bloom. Either hose herbs down gently with water the night before you gather them, or rinse them after picking, and then blot away any moisture. For best results, prepare plants for drying immediately after harvesting.

THE BASICS OF DRYING

To dry properly, plants need circulating air (preferably warm, dry air) and a darkened room, such as an attic, shed, or garage free of car fumes. In a damp, still room, mold will grow on the plants. Sunlight robs petals of their colors and some herbs of their flavors. Drying times range from a few hours to 10 weeks, depending on the amount of moisture in the plant and the drying method used. Six days is usually adequate for drying most herbs, as long as the humidity is low and the temperature is between 70°F and 90°F (21°C and 32°C). If herbs are dried much longer, they may lose their flavors.

HANGING

Hanging is the simplest way to dry aromatics and herbs, and it allows them to dry in the most natural position. Just secure several stems of one type of plant together with a rubber band, and then hang the bunch upside down by attaching it to a nail or rope with a paper clip opened to an S-shape or with a clothes pin. (Avoid tying the bundles with string; stems shrink as they dry, and unless you retighten the string regularly, the stems will slip out.) To dry large quantities in this manner, mount a length of lightweight chain from one side of your drying room to the other, and hook the paper clips into its links. This will keep the bunches evenly separated. Blooms and leaves are dry when they feel papery and rigid.

Rosemary

SCREEN DRYING

Screen drying is suitable for fragile stems, large flower heads, or loose petals. Window screens work well. Just raise them off the floor or ground by setting them on bricks so that air can circulate around them. Making a screen is easy. Build or buy a wooden frame and staple a piece of hardware cloth across its top. When screen drying, you need to turn your materials every day or two to prevent curling. For large flower blossoms, punch a hole in the screen, remove leaves from the stem, and stick the stem down through the screen, allowing the head to remain flared open against the screen's flat surface. If you're drying loose petals, turn them once every few days.

OVEN DRYING

For flowers with many petals, preheat an oven to 175°F (80°C) and place the flowers—still attached to their stems—directly on the oven racks. To maintain the flavor of culinary herbs, make sure the oven temperature never exceeds 150°F (65°C). Leave the oven door cracked open, and remove the items before they're completely dry. This drying method can take anywhere from three to ten hours, depending on the moisture content of the flowers. After removing the flowers from the oven, place them on a rack or screen to complete the drying process.

PRESSING

To press, you simply place your plant between sheets of newspaper, wax paper, or blotting paper; set the sheets on a hard surface; and weigh them down with several heavy books. In two to four weeks, carefully uncover the plant. The paper will have absorbed the plant's moisture, leaving you a delicate whisper of a plant.

DEHYDRATOR DRYING

For perfect drying, the electric dehydrator is unmatched. These energy-efficient devices circulate heated air evenly, usually through stacked trays, and are particularly useful for drying flowers with numerous petals, such as rose buds. Available through mail-order suppliers and some hardware stores, they're well worth their cost, especially if you'd also like to dry fruits and vegetables.

STORING DRIED PLANTS

Store dried herbs and other aromatics out of the sun, in pottery or darkened glass containers with airtight lids. (Paper bags and plastic containers can leach away desirable oils.) In general, properly dried and stored herbs will keep for 12 to 18 months.

To create a fragrant potpourri, simply blend a mixture of fragrant dried naturals, and add a fixative such as orris root or cellulose fibers—both available from health-food stores—to extend the life of the fragrance. When the aroma begins to fade, leave the mixture in a humid room, where the moisture will release more fragrance.

Golden thyme

Lavender

Golden sage

Drying Aromatics

AROMATIC PLANT	HARVESTING METHOD	DRYING METHODS
Basil *Ocimum basilicum*	harvest stems with leaves before plant blooms	screen drying (turn plant frequently), hanging in small bunches; leaves will shrink 50%
Bee balm *Monarda didyma*	harvest stems with blooms and leaves just as flowers open	hang in small bunches; leaves will shrink 50%
Chamomile *Chamaemelum nobile*	harvest flowers when fully opened; pick leaves at any time	screen drying, hanging, pressing, or upright in a vase
Lavender *Lavandula angustifolia*	harvest spikes at full bloom	screen drying, hanging, pressing, or upright in a vase
Lemon balm *Melissa officinalis*	harvest stems with leaves at any time	screen drying, hanging in small bunches, pressing; leaves will shrink 60%
Lemon verbena *Aloysia triphylla*	harvest blooms when just beginning to open; pick leaves at any time	screen drying, hanging in small bunches, pressing
Rose *Rosa*	harvest when buds are tight or slightly opened	screen drying or pressing (petals), oven (whole flower), or dehydrator
Rosemary *Rosmarinus officinalis*	pick leaves at any time but preferably during flowering	screen drying (small sprigs), hanging (long stems), pressing
Sage *Salvia officinalis*	harvest blooms at their peak; pick leaves at any time	screen drying, hanging, pressing; plant retains 75% of fragrance
Thyme *Thymus*	harvest stems with leaves before plant blooms for best flavor	screen drying, hanging in small buches, pressing; leaves retain much of their fragrance

An Aromatic Window Box Plan

Throw open your window and let the clean, fresh scent of aromatics into your home. Reach out and snip a few stems of thyme to flavor a stew or some fragrant lavender to add to your bath. A window box is the perfect place for a miniature aromatic garden.

Just be sure to situate the box so it receives at least six hours of sun each day. Keep the plants well watered (soil dries out more quickly in containers than in the ground); occasional harvesting should keep them from becoming leggy or overrunning the box.

A ROMAN CHAMOMILE
Chamaemelum nobile

Hardiness zones 6–9

1 to 6 inches tall

Small, white, daisy-like flowers with golden centers late spring to early fall; bright green, ferny foliage; dry, well-drained soil; full sun to light shade; leaves release apple scent when crushed

B SWEET ALYSSUM
Lobularia

Annual

4 to 12 inches tall

Tiny, fragrant, white, pink, or purple flowers from late spring to frost; narrow, lance-shaped, light to mid-green leaves; well-drained soil; full sun to partial shade; flowers release a refreshing honey-like scent

C LAVENDER
Lavandula angustifolia 'Munstead'

Hardiness zones 5–10

up to 18 inches tall

Whorls of fragrant blue-purple, flowers atop long stems in mid to late summer; linear, gray-green foliage; well-drained to dry soil; full sun; flowers release fresh, clean scent

D HELIOTROPE
Heliotropium

Hardiness zones 10–11

up to 18 inches (in a container)

Large clusters of tiny, sweetly scented, deep purple to white flowers in summer; oval to lance-shaped mid- to dark green leaves; well-drained, fertile soil; full sun to partial shade; flowers release a sweet vanilla scent

E ROSEMARY
Rosmarinus officinalis
'Miss Jessopp's Upright'

Hardiness zones 8–10

up to 5 feet tall (if grown outdoors in zones 8–10)

Tiny, pale blue, tubular flowers from midspring to early summer; fragrant, needlelike leaves used in cooking; well-drained, alkaline soil; full sun; buy small plant for window box (may be over-wintered inside in pot on sunny windowsill)

F THYME
Thymus

Hardiness zones 3–9

2 to 18 inches tall

Small clusters of pink, purple, or white flowers in summer; tiny, aromatic leaves used in cooking; well-drained, alkaline soil; full sun; fresh, pungent scent

Edible Flowers

Noshing on flowers may seem trendy, but it's actually an ancient culinary tradition. Flowers have been valued as attractive, flavorful ingredients since before Roman times. Today, flowers are making a comeback as food and can be found snuggled up next to lettuce in restaurant salads and alongside the produce in gourmet grocery stores. Many flowers you may be growing in your backyard are edible (daylilies, Johnny-jump-ups, roses,

pansies, and hollyhocks are just a few). While some are quite bland and valued more for their color than their taste, others are sweet, spicy, or even peppery. Sometimes the taste of a flower varies, depending on both the variety and where and how the plant was grown.

Flower garnishes lend an elegant, festive touch to any meal, but the blooms can do more than sit prettily on top of food. Next time you plan to serve grilled meat or seafood, try

blending a colorful confetti of chopped nasturtium petals with butter to make a delicious spread. In rice dishes, calendula petals make a great substitute for costly saffron. Both lavender and rose are subtle flavor additives for cookie and ice cream recipes. Daylily buds may be stir fried or dipped in batter and deep fried. Raw daylily buds are tasty, especially when they're stuffed with nuts and cream cheese. And don't forget flowers in drinks. Freeze them in ice cubes or float them in the top of a punch bowl to turn any occasion into a party. Candied flowers (brush the petals with egg whites mixed with a little water and then sprinkle on granulated sugar) look lovely on cakes and cookies.

HARVESTING FLOWERS

Harvest flowers early in the morning. Select only blooms that are free of insect damage and disease. Placing the blossoms between damp paper towels in a plastic bag and refrigerating the bag will help keep the flowers fresh for several days, but flowers taste and look best when they're used the day they're picked. Wash harvested flowers in lukewarm water, checking carefully for bugs. Just before you use the

blossoms, plunge them quickly into ice water to revive them.

FLOWER SAFETY

Although some flowers are culinary delights, others are downright dangerous to eat, so don't dash outdoors and pop the first flower you see into your mouth. While many flowers are perfectly safe and even nutritious (violets are high in vitamin C and beta-carotene), you do want to take some common sense precautions when eating flowers.

Eat only flowers that you are certain are safe; don't assume flowers are safe just because they're served with food: Even restaurants have made the mistake of serving toxic blossoms.

People with asthma or allergies should not eat flowers. Blossoms from florists, gardening centers, or home gardens that use pesticides aren't safe for consumption, and neither are flowers that grow along roadsides.

Only the petals of most flowers are edible; remove the pistils and stamens before tasting or serving the rest of the blossom. And start with only small amounts of any new flower; eating too much may upset your stomach. If you'd like to cultivate your own crop of edibles, start them from seed and grow them organically. A kitchen window box or container on the patio might be a convenient spot for your first foray into edible flower gardening.

THE FLAVORS OF FLOWERS

Some flowers are fairly bland and contribute mainly color and texture to food while others add a distinct flavor. Tastes are described for the flowers shown below, clockwise, from top left.

Stock *Matthiola incana*	bland, use as garnish
Calendula *Calendula officinalis*	peppery
Bachelor's-button *Centaurea cyanus*	bland, use as a garnish
Snapdragon *Antirrhinum majus*	slightly sweet
Scented geranium *Pelargonium*	flavor depends on variety
Nasturtium *Tropaeolum majus*	spicy, peppery, somewhat like watercress
Pansy *Viola x Wittrockiana*	somewhat like lettuce
Johnny-jump-up *Viola tricolor*	mild wintergreen
Hollyhock *Alcea rosea*	somewhat like lettuce

Miniature Backyard Orchards

When pristine, shiny, red and green apples are so easy to purchase, why should home gardeners consider planting orchards? The answer is simple: The best-tasting apples—and hundreds of varieties exist—are often excluded from produce bins simply because their skins aren't flaming red or flawless green and because they can't be stored for months on end. Selecting and growing your own varieties will introduce you to an entirely new world of apple flavors.

If you thought you couldn't grow apples because you didn't have the space, you'll be delighted by today's mini-dwarf (or miniature) trees, which can be set as close as six feet apart and which rarely exceed six to eight feet in height. These tiny versions of standard-sized trees bear full-sized fruit— at a height that makes harvesting and maintenance a breeze. Just imagine stepping out your back door next spring to a low-floating cloud of delicate, fragrant blossoms.

PREPARATIONS

As you select a site for your miniature orchard, keep in mind that apple trees do best on gentle, sunny, south-facing slopes, where cold air drains down and away from them. Avoid low-lying and shaded areas. Also make sure not to plant within ten feet of sidewalks or

buried water, sewer, or electrical lines.

Although apple trees will grow in a fairly wide range of soil types, they do require a well-drained site and won't survive in heavy clays. Loosen soil with a moderate clay content by adding peat, sand, and plenty of composted organic material. Test the soil first and add amendments as necessary, well in advance of planting.

SELECTING APPLE VARIETIES

The apple trees sold today consist of two parts that are grafted together: An upper portion known as the *scion* (which eventually branches out and bears fruit) and the lower portion—or *rootstock*—which controls the size of the tree. The scion determines the variety of apple that the tree will produce.

Because most apple trees require cross-pollination in order to bear fruit, you must plant at least two different varieties in close proximity to each other. (Make sure that the two varieties you select will blossom at the same time.) A few varieties produce sterile pollen, and so cannot be used as pollinizers; by all means include these in your orchard, but make sure you plant at least two pollinizing varieties as well. Before making your final selections, ask your Cooperative Extension Service or nursery for advice regarding the best varieties for your growing area. Bees transfer pollen from one tree to another, so avoid

using any garden pesticides when your trees are blooming.

PLANTING APPLE TREES

Apple trees are sold in three different ways: *Bare-rooted* (without soil around their roots), in containers, or with balled roots (the roots and soil are wrapped in burlap). Soak the roots of bare-rooted trees for several hours just before planting.

Remove all sod and weeds from the planting site. Next, dig a hole for each tree, spacing the holes six feet apart and making each one twice as wide as the extended tree roots. If the trees are bare-rooted, make a small, conical mound of soil in the hole—one high enough to hold the tree's graft union about two inches above ground level. Then spread the roots down and around the mound and add topsoil

(don't add fertilizer) until the hole is two-thirds full. Pack the soil firmly, water the tree well, and finish filling the hole with soil. Don't leave a depression around the trunk; water that freezes around the trunk will kill the tree. Water again when you're finished, lifting the tree up and down slightly to settle the soil around the roots. You'll also need to cut the tree back; the nursery that provides your trees should also provide planting and pruning instructions.

If your trees arrive with burlap-wrapped balls of soil around their roots, untie and discard the rope that fastens the burlap to the trunk. Set the root ball in the hole with the burlap loosely around it (no interior mound of soil is necessary), and fill the hole as before. The burlap will gradually disintegrate. Plant trees purchased in containers in the same way, but remove them from the containers first, and follow the nursery's instructions regarding root pruning.

EARLY CARE

Remove any tags, so they won't strangle the trees as they grow. Protect the tender trunks by surrounding each one with a tree wrap or guard, both available at nurseries. To prevent the injuries that result when the trunks absorb too much heat during the winter, paint the trunks with a water-soluble white latex paint diluted with water in a 1:1 ratio.

The rootstocks of miniature apple trees are weak, so you'll need to use permanent stakes. Set each stake about three inches from the tree, and tie it to the trunk. Check the ties frequently

and loosen them as necessary to prevent strangling.

Water the newly planted trees once every week when the weather is dry. Water until the soil is moist to a depth of 12 to 18 inches. After their first growing season, the trees won't require much watering unless your region is suffering from drought.

PRUNING

The art of pruning apple trees is one that requires some study, but most nurseries provide instructional brochures with the trees they sell, and your local Cooperative Extension Service can also give excellent pruning advice. The primary goal of pruning is to guide the tree's growth. Each main trunk should have a single upright limb (or leader) at its top, and a series of

sturdy, radiating branches known as laterals, which extend out from the trunk in different compass directions, about four to six inches apart on the trunk.

MAINTENANCE

Cultivate the soil each spring, removing all grass and weeds in a three-foot diameter circle around each tree. Cover the soil with several inches of mulch during the summer (don't let the mulch touch the trunks), and remove the mulch during the winter. Unless you choose to care for your orchard organically (a difficult proposition), follow the fertilization and spraying programs recommended by your nursery or extension agent.

HARVESTING

To help the trees direct their energy to the development of laterals until the fourth year, remove all fruit as soon as each apple is the size of a dime. During the fourth season, your orchard will be ready to harvest. Some immature fruit will drop to the ground, usually during June. (This June drop will occur every year once the trees have reached maturity.) Thin out the remaining fruit until the apples are at least eight inches apart on the branches. They'll be ready to pick when their seeds are brown and when they twist easily away from the branches. You can expect to harvest about one-quarter of a bushel of apples per tree.

A Miniature Orchard Plan

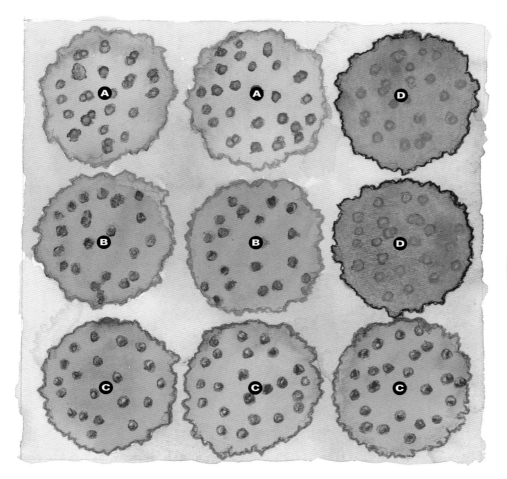

If you plant them six feet apart and keep them pruned to six feet in height, the trees in the orchard plan presented above will take up an area only eighteen feet square. The varieties selected will provide you with apples that are good for eating fresh, for cooking, and for making cider. What's more, each variety will ripen at a different time, so you'll have plenty of fruit from early to late autumn.

A DISCOVERY
Hardiness zones 4–8

Best uses: Best early-season apple for fresh eating and cooking; prolific producer and very reliable
Color: Yellow-tan with splashes of bright pinkish-red
Flesh: Creamy smooth, white with streaks of pink. If well ripened on the tree, can develop to crisp and juicy with a hint of strawberry flavor
Bloomtime: Mid season
Harvest time: Mid August
Resistance: A little to scab

B HONEY CRISP
Hardiness zones 3–8

Best uses: Good fresh eating, cooking, and dessert apple; tremendous keeper—up to 5 months in storage
Color: Mottled red over a yellow background
Flesh: Very crisp, juicy, sweet, with slight acidity
Bloomtime: Mid season
Harvest time: Early October
Resistance: Fireblight and scab

C LIBERTY
Hardiness zones 4–8

Best uses: Fresh eating, cooking, and dessert apple; good keeper; spurs profusely so always produces fruit no matter how badly you treat it
Color: 90% red marble blush over a yellow background
Flesh: Creamy white with a coarse, juicy sweet, slight subacid flavor
Bloomtime: Early season
Harvest time: Early October
Resistance: Immune to apple scab, highly resistant to cedar apple rust, fireblight, and powdery mildew

D GRIMES GOLDEN
Hardiness zones 5–9

Best uses: Dessert, juice, and cider apple; good keeper; good pollinator
Color: Bright golden, yellowish-green fruit
Flesh: Rich golden-yellow color with a sweet, crisp, honeyed, and juicy flavor
Bloomtime: Mid season
Harvest time: Late October

Escaping the Sun

Although we may not want to admit it, many of us fall into the same rut: We dream all winter about relaxing in our lush, verdant backyards; we spend all spring slavishly cultivating those fabulous yards; and then pass the summer indoors, with the air conditioners on full blast, dreaming about . . . last winter. What we need is shade—cool, soothing, shade—and it's easier to get than you might think.

Plant the right tree in a strategic spot, and before long, its circle of leafy shade will become a favorite spot in your yard. For quicker shade, hoist an awning or umbrella over your patio or deck so you can dine or relax while sheltered from the sun. Or perhaps you'd like to add a graceful gazebo or pergola to your yard, so that each time you step outside you feel as if you're on vacation. For the ultimate sun escape, plant a bed of night-blooming flowers that wait until after sunset to release their heady fragrances and then glow in the moonlight.

Don't fret about not being able to grow gorgeous plants in all this newly created shade. Some of the most stunning botanical specimens thrive where you'll actually be inspired to tend to them—in the coolest, most welcoming part of your yard.

Shade Trees

Planting a tree is not the quickest way to get shade in your yard, but it may be the smartest. Did you know that the temperature beneath a shade tree can be a full 15°F (8°C) degrees cooler than in a sunny site? Did you know that as few as three properly situated trees can cut your air-conditioning bills in half?

No other plant can perform so many functions at one time. A well-tended tree gives your home a feeling of permanence and actually increases the value of your property when you sell your house. It can hide unattractive views while buffering traffic noise. It will absorb carbon dioxide and replenish oxygen. Its roots will combat soil erosion while acting as a natural filter for pollutants. A tree's leaves (which also filter pollution) will add organic nutrients to your soil. Trees provide habitats for wildlife and at the same time add vertical elements to your landscape design. Without a doubt, the right tree in the right place is a wonderful addition to your yard, but the wrong tree in the wrong place can be a costly mistake, so it pays to plan carefully before planting.

CHOOSING A SHADE TREE

The best shade trees are round or vase shaped, deciduous, and deep-rooted. Deciduous trees block the hot summer sun but allow the warming sun of winter through. Deep-rooted trees, such as honey locusts, oaks, and loblolly pines won't compete with nearby plants. If you're planning on growing plants beneath the tree, avoid trees with dense canopies of large leaves. Instead, choose finer-leaved trees such as honey locusts; these cast dappled shade in which plants can grow.

While fast-growing trees (such as poplars) provide shade quickly, they tend to be short-lived, and their wood is more vulnerable to damage from insects, diseases, and storms than the wood of slower growing trees. Local nurseries or your Cooperative Extension Service should be able to tell you which shade trees grow best in your climate and your particular site.

PURCHASING SHADE TREES

Trees are among the costliest plants to purchase (and the larger they are, the more expensive they'll be), but think of them as long-term, low-maintenance investments. Select healthy, vigorous trees, at least five to six feet tall, with a two-inch caliper (the perimeter of the stem six inches above the ground). Avoid trees with damaged bark. You can purchase trees as bareroot, with balled roots wrapped in burlap, or in containers. Make sure you leave the

nursery with specific planting instructions for your type of tree.

PLANTING AND CARE OF SHADE TREES

To find the best site for your shade tree, study the movement of the sun across your yard, keeping in mind that the pattern will change throughout the year. If you'd like to shade a specific part of your yard, such as a terrace, be sure to plant the tree so it will shade that spot during the hottest time of day (or during the time you're most likely to use the area). In general, shade trees should be located on the south or southwest side of your house or yard. If you plan to grow flowering plants near your tree, situate the tree so that your flowers will receive morning sun and afternoon shade. As you select a site, consider the spread of the mature tree's roots and branches, too; make sure they won't interfere with overhead or underground utilities.

How you should plant your tree will depend, in part, on whether you purchased the tree bareroot, burlapped, or in a container; get detailed instructions from the nursery or your Cooperative Extension Service. In general, start by digging a hole as deep and at least twice as wide as the root ball. Then set the tree at the same depth that it grew in the nursery (the soil line should be obvious on the tree trunk); spread the roots out; and prune back

any broken ones. Fill the hole halfway with topsoil, and water well. Refill the hole entirely and water until the soil is moist to a depth of 12 to 18 inches. Cover the bare dirt with a two- to three-inch layer of mulch, but don't let the mulch touch the trunk.

Most trees only need to be staked if they're more than eight feet tall, are top heavy, or are being planted in a windy location. To protect tree trunks from gnawing animals, sun damage, and nicks from lawnmowers, place a loose-fitting plastic tree wrap or wire guard around the trunk.

Your new tree will need regular deep watering for one full year after planting. A top-dressing of compost (see page 114) is all the fertilization most trees require.

Umbrellas and Awnings

A ll through the spring, you've dug, planted, and weeded around your patio, spurred on by visions of alfresco dinners in your beautiful backyard. Now summer is in its fullness, the yard is indeed lovely, and yet you find yourself choosing to eat most meals indoors because "it's just too hot out there." Consider the solutions to this problem; they're easier than you might think.

UMBRELLAS

A patio umbrella will cast shade where you want it—when you want it—while adding a splash of color to your yard. The typical patio umbrella extends from five to nine feet in diameter above a pole that runs through a hole in your tabletop and is anchored by a weighted aluminum or concrete base. A crank usually raises and lowers the umbrella. Patio umbrellas can also come free-standing for use without a table, and some are as large as 20 feet in diameter.

One of your first decisions will be to choose the fabric: cotton or acrylic. Well-made acrylic fabric manufactured with a solution-dyeing process will prove far more resistant to fading and mildew than cotton, which—while less expensive—will quickly prove itself to be a fair-weather friend. Solution-dyed acrylic repels moisture at the surface, while cotton fabrics (even when waterproofed) will usually allow some moisture through. With both acrylic and cotton, mildew can grow on dirt and other organic material that attaches itself to the fabric, so spot washing your umbrella regularly is a good idea.

Of course, you'll also want to pick a style and color of umbrella that complements, rather than clashes with, your home and yard. Standard patio umbrellas tend to come in solid colors or stripes. More expensive umbrellas offer you a wider choice of sizes and patterns.

When purchasing umbrellas, look for sturdy frames made from heavy-gauge aluminum or hardwoods such as ash and mahogany. If you buy a foreign-made product, make sure the wood is an equivalent of the American hardwoods. Poles that are constructed by screwing together separate pieces may be easier to ship, but they're also less stable than solid ones. If you want the pole to fit a standard umbrella table, make sure it's two inches or less in width.

An umbrella with a tilting mechanism will allow you more sun-blocking options, but make sure the model you select is well built and stable. (The hardware, cable, pins, and screws of all umbrellas should be steel or brass.) Umbrellas raised with rope cords rather than steel cables and those held together with flimsy hardware may only see you through a few summers. Umbrellas raised and lowered with double pulley systems will usually outlast all others.

Whatever final product you select, insure a longer lifetime for your umbrella by keeping it closed when it's not in use and storing it inside during rainstorms and colder seasons.

AWNINGS

If you'd like to shade more than just a table or small area, consider adding an awning to your home. An awning can transform the look of any patio or deck, while providing a visual transition between indoors and out and filtering out harmful ultraviolet radiation. But the primary reason you might opt for an awning is energy efficiency. On a hot summer day, an awning can reduce temperatures of adjacent rooms by a whopping 15°F (8°C). If you typically pay high air-conditioning bills, one of these more expensive sun shields could eventually pay for itself.

Unlike umbrellas, awnings have a very real impact on your house's architecture—make sure you choose a style that enhances both your house and yard. A brick red awning on a Spanish-style house will place it firmly along the Mediterranean coast. A candy-striped awning will lend a cheerful touch to your home. Remember that you will probably be able to see the inside of the awning from at least part of your home, so consider, too, the style and colors of those rooms when choosing your awning.

Since an awning is usually a much larger purchase than an umbrella, it's even more important to determine the quality of an awning's fabric, frame, and mechanisms. Make sure all materials are weatherproof and sturdy and the construction is solid. Before you buy your awning, familiarize yourself with the warranty the manufacturer provides and the options available to you for replacing the fabric.

Typically, awnings must be left exposed to the elements; one alternative is an awning that can be retracted (either manually or with a motor) to avoid inclement weather or when sun is desired. Some even come equipped with sun and wind sensors that automatically activate the lifting mechanisms.

Pergolas

O h, dear. Have you made your yard so lovely that now you can't bear to be away for even a couple of weeks? Don't worry. Why not sip iced cappuccinos in the leafy shade of your own backyard pergola—and buy more plants with the money you save on airfare to Italy?

Pergolas (sometimes called arbors) are structures with open roofs supported by columns. As well as casting shade, pergolas provide a place to grow all manner of climbing, twining, rambling, and scrambling vines. Built over a path, a pergola creates a covered walkway; sheltering a patio or deck, it provides an outdoor "room" for dining or entertaining. Though pergolas range in style from stately to rustic, sitting or strolling beneath one will make you feel as if you're vacationing in a private Mediterranean villa.

CHOOSING A PERGOLA

If your yard includes a walkway that might benefit from the play of light and shade or the addition of a vertical element, a tunnel-like pergola may be in order. If you'd like a shady bower beneath which you can dine or relax, a larger pergola (either freestanding or attached to one wall of your house) will work well.

Like all garden structures, pergolas are both functional and ornamental.

While choosing one that won't collapse in a windstorm or buckle under a heavy snow should be your first priority, you'll also want to choose one that won't clash with the style or color of your house. (This is especially true if the pergola will actually be an attached extension to the house.) A cedar-sided home surrounded by native plants might call for a rustic pergola made with locust poles.

A more formal house would be enhanced by a white wooden pergola with classic lines and columns. The materials—whether wood, brick, stone, or metal—should match or be compatible with those of your house. Lattice, wood 2 x 2s or 2 x 4s, woven reed, bamboo, and even canvas are all possible roofing options. When it comes to choosing roof materials, remember that the size and spacing of the materials will affect the type of shade beneath.

Although it's possible to build a pergola that's too large and that overwhelms the house or yard, don't be cowardly when it comes to "thinking big." You'd be surprised by how much a space will seem to shrink once you set up a table and a few chairs. And any pergola-covered pathway will be much more user-friendly if two people can walk abreast along the path without being scratched by rose thorns or swatted by wet leaves. No matter what size pergola you choose, before you progress too far with your plans, check with local officials regarding building codes that might apply to your new structure, and find out whether or not a building permit is required.

SELECTING A SITE

A pergola should cast shade where and when you want it most, so familiarize yourself with the sun's path across your yard. And as you study the path, remember that the sun's position and angle change continually throughout the year. If you're planning to construct a pergola to shelter a path, try to place it so that an attractive goal, such as a bench or small pond, will be visible at the path's end. Strollers will be much more likely to use the path if there's something that draws them along it.

The open "walls" of a pergola that covers a terrace or deck will form visual frames for your yard, so make sure you like the pictures at which you'll be gazing. Also, take care that any pergola attached to your house doesn't block a lovely view from indoors or prevent desired sunlight from reaching your home's interior.

PLANTS FOR PERGOLAS

Few experiences can match the opulence of relaxing beneath a canopy of fragrant wisteria in full bloom or sipping wine on a terrace as clusters of grapes dangle overhead. So many wonderful plants can grow up and over pergolas that you may find yourself building a few more for your yard!

For pergolas located close to a house, deciduous climbers are best; their leaves will provide summer shade, but will die back to allow light and warmth to filter through in winter. Perfumed plants, such as jasmine and honeysuckle, can be lovely overhead, but too much of a good thing *is* possible, especially near dining areas—floral perfumes don't always mix well with the aromas and flavors of food. Also, make sure the vines you choose will actually grow tall enough to climb up the posts and over the top of your shelter. Your choice of plants will sometimes be determined by the sturdiness of your pergola. Wisteria and trumpet vine, for example, grow too vigorously for all but the most substantial of supporting structures.

Wisteria

10 Plants for Pergolas

- **Clematis**
  Clematis

- **Climbing hydrangea**
  Hydrangea petiolaris

- **Climbing roses**
  Rosa

- **Grape vine**
  Vitis

- **Jasmine**
  Jasminum

- **Malabar gourd**
  Cucurbita ficifolia

- **Moonflower**
  Ipomoea alba

- **Scarlet honeysuckle**
  Lonicera sempervirens

- **Trumpet vine**
  Campsis radicans

- **Wisteria**
  Wisteria

Gazebos

Few garden features are as romantic as gazebos. Even the word itself (thought by some to be a combination of *gaze* and *about*) sounds whimsical. But there is a practical side to these poetic structures: A gazebo can become an extra room for your home. Picture yourself reading in its shade on a lazy summer afternoon—or lingering over dinner with friends inside a screened gazebo as the children dance after fireflies in the yard.

PLANNING

A gazebo is a structure that will alter the whole character of your yard, so it's important to plan thoroughly before installing one. Research legalities such as building codes, zoning ordinances, and your property deed. Then consider your needs. Do you want an extra space for entertaining or do you just need a place to rest in the shade while gardening? Do you want to be able to use the gazebo on rainy days?

Look in magazines and books for pictures of gazebos that appeal to you. Most are round or octagonal, but some are rectangular or three-sided. Pick a style that blends in with the design elements of your home and garden. For example, if you have a shingle roof on your home, tie in the gazebo by roofing it in shingles. If you live in a timber frame home, complement the structure by building a gazebo crafted with dovetailed joinery and wooden pegs.

Next, take some graph paper and create a map of your house and yard drawn to scale. Include trees, garden areas, and the property line. Show where the windows and doors are on the house. Indicate the direction of the sun and the location of utility lines and any wet spots in your yard.

Now use this map to determine the best position for a gazebo. Place tracing paper over the map and draw in the gazebo roof top, experimenting with different locations. It should be accessible to foot traffic and should not block desired views from any of your windows. Gazebos work best as a design element when they are positioned at the edges of gardens, defining a boundary and leaving the middle open for planting and recreation. A gazebo built in the center of a yard can sometimes look exposed and out of place. It will not seem as inviting as it would if it were placed to the side and landscaped into the yard with shrubbery and climbing vines, appearing as though it had always been there.

Plan the site carefully, taking water drainage into account. You may need to consult a soil engineer and a structural engineer before the foundation is built if you live on an unstable slope or in a windy region. They can insure that the foundation is well matched to the soil it rests upon.

Once you've settled on the site, you can gauge the gazebo's dimensions. A general rule is to build a gazebo as large as possible while keeping it balanced with its surroundings.

BUILDING THE GAZEBO

Use only the finest materials, and build a sturdy gazebo meant to last. If you try to cut corners on quality, you'll end up with an expensive eyesore. The most popular material for gazebos is wood, but other materials include glass or plastic for roofs and windows; tiles, shingles, and aluminum for roofs; steel, stucco, and concrete for posts.

If you decide to hire a professional builder to construct your gazebo, get recommendations from gazebo owners or ask a trade association for names. Some gazebo builders will let you customize their stock designs.

Many people opt for gazebo kits, which range quite a bit in price. Before purchasing a kit, it is wise to look at a finished model and to scrutinize the instructions for clarity. You should also find out what kind of wood is in the kit and how it needs to be finished. Make sure you know exactly what is included in the kit, such as screening and flooring, and who is to cover the cost of delivery.

If you hire a carpenter to assemble the kit, the project will still be less expensive than if you had the gazebo designed and constructed by a builder. You can also have the carpenter tailor the kit to your own design.

PLANTING THE GAZEBO

One of the best ways to blend the edges of a gazebo into its surroundings is to plant vines or climbing plants around it. Consult a nursery to see which ones would do best in your region. Consider wisteria, grapes, clematis, climbing roses, trumpet vine, or bougainvillea, depending on the microclimate of your gazebo's site.

Shade Gardening

Perhaps those trees you planted a few years back grew a little taller a little faster than you'd anticipated. Or perhaps you've bought a house blessed with mature plantings and a lot of shade. Does this mean you'll have to give up on gardening? Certainly not: A surprising number of plants can glorify your shady spots with myriad shapes, heights, textures, and a rainbow of colors.

MADE IN THE SHADE

While it's true many flowering plants need full to partial sun, it's also true that there's plenty to be grateful for if you're gardening in shade. You can get away with less watering, mulching, weeding, and pruning than when gardening in full sun. Some garden pests, such as slugs and snails, prefer shade, but many of the most damaging insects (aphids, mites, and caterpillars, for instance) will number far fewer in shade gardens. And come late July, you'll find yourself much more willing to be out maintaining shade gardens than toiling beneath the scorching sun.

Gardeners in warm climates can grow many "full sun" plants in afternoon shade. Shade will also turn you into a more sophisticated gardener. Because fewer flowering plants grow in shade, you'll need to concentrate on texture, size, and shape when choosing plants—all elements essential to a well-designed garden. Once you discover the elegant beauty of a fern frond unfolding or the handsome composition a planting of stately hostas can offer, a whole new world of gardening will open up to you.

GARDENING IN THE SHADE

Okay, you're convinced there's a sunny side to shade gardening; now, how do you go about doing it? Well, the first thing you need to figure out is just what kind of shade you are dealing with. Full shade areas receive no direct sunlight at all. Areas with partial shade receive sun for four to six hours a day. Gardens with dappled shade usually get only sunlight that filters through the foliage of trees. It *is* difficult to grow a large variety of plants in full shade, but many plants thrive in partial or dappled shade.

Of course, the shade in your yard will shift continuously as the sun moves from east to west each day, as the sun's position in the sky changes throughout the year, and as the tall plants in your yard grow or die.

You can usually alter at least some of the shade in your yard. Large trees can be pruned to thin their leafy canopies, and dark walls may be painted white or another light color to better reflect light. If you have the advantage of choosing your planting areas, remember that morning sun and afternoon shade is a better combination for plants than morning shade and afternoon sun. (Morning sun will help dry the dew from plants, and afternoon shade will provide relief from the harshest sun of the day.)

PLANTS FOR SHADE

A large assortment of flowering shrubs grows in shade. The enchanting blue blossoms of a lace-cap hydrangea will cheer up any dark corner of your yard, while the electric orange blooms of a flame azalea will practically shout. Many shade shrubs also

Astilbe

offer berries or variegated foliage, and some, such as witch hazel and daphne, will scent your yard with their wonderful fragrances.

You'll probably run out of room in your shaded areas well before you run out of varieties of perennials that would grow there. Many woodland wildflowers, such as cardinal flower and lupine, thrive in partial shade. Plants such as Jack-in-the-pulpit and Solomon's seal add their own unique beauty to any garden. And gardeners in warm climates with partial or dappled shade can try out a host of perennials that are sun-lovers in colder climates.

Of course, when it comes to shade annuals, the old stand-bys, impatiens and begonias, are readily available at most gardening centers, but you can also liven up your dark spots with the colorful wishbone flower (*Torenia*),

fragrant flowering tobacco, or the tall spires of foxgloves (usually biennial). Fuchsia, ageratum, and evening primrose are all flowering annuals that perform well in shade.

The hardest part of growing ground covers in shaded sections of your yard may be selecting from among the many choices available. Periwinkle, pachysandra, ajuga, ivy, and moss are just a few of the many low-growing, fast-spreading plants that prefer shade.

When you buy plants for your shade areas, choose the fullest ones you can find, since plants tend to grow leggier in shade. Purchase the earliest blooming varieties of annuals, perennials, and bulbs if you will be planting them under deciduous trees. And finally, look for varieties with variegated foliage to add even more bright highlights to your shade gardens.

A Shade Garden Plan

W ork with, rather than fighting, Mother Nature to let the shady sections of your yard add their own charm and beauty to your property. All of the plants in this garden will thrive in partial shade. The plants' flowers, though subtle, will embellish this shade bed off and on from spring to fall; while the hues, textures, and variegations of the plants' foliage brighten the shady spot all season long. Because this bed is planted beneath a deciduous tree (in this instance, a birch), early-flowering bulbs could also be added to the bed.

A WOOD FERN
Dryopteris
Hardiness zones 4–8
1 to 2 feet tall
Leathery green leaves used for textural accent; moist, well-drained soil; filtered sun to full shade

B 'FRANCEE' HOSTA
Hosta 'Francee'
Hardiness zones 3–9
24 inches tall
Funnel-shaped, lavender blue flowers in summer; large, heart-shaped, puckered, green leaves with irregular, white margins; fertile, moist, well-drained soil; partial to full shade

C 'GOLD STANDARD' HOSTA
Hosta 'Gold Standard'
Hardiness zones 3–9
24 inches tall
Funnel-shaped, pale lavender flowers in summer; heart-shaped, chartreuse leaves with irregular, dark green margins; fertile, moist, well-drained soil; partial to full shade

D BISHOP'S WEED
Aegopodium podagraria 'Variegatum'
Hardiness zones 3–10
up to 12 inches tall
Flat clusters of white flowers late spring to early summer; deep green leaves with irregular, creamy white margins; tolerates dry or moist, poor soil; partial shade to full sun; can be invasive if not contained

E 'ELEGANS' HOSTA
Hosta 'Elegans'
Hardiness zones 3–9
36 inches tall
Funnel-shaped, lavender-white flowers in summer; large, heart-shaped, dark blue-green leaves; fertile, moist, well-drained soil; partial to full shade

F BLEEDING HEART
Dicentra spectabilis
Hardiness zones 3–8
up to 48 inches tall
Heart-shaped, pink and white flowers dangling from arched stems late spring to early summer; lacy, pale green leaves; moist, well-drained soil; partial shade

G GRAPE-LEAVED ANEMONE
Anemone vitifolia 'Robustissima'
Hardiness zones 3–8
up to 36 inches tall
Clusters of small, mauve-pink flowers held high above foliage in late summer and early autumn; dark green leaves are white and woolly underneath; fertile, moist soil; sun or partial shade

H OAKLEAF HYDRANGEA
Hydrangea quercifolia
Hardiness zones 5–9
up to 6 feet tall
White flowers in conical clusters early to late summer; large leaves, resembling oak leaves, turn crimson in autumn; moist, well-drained soil; partial shade

A Moonlight Garden

A poet once said that the two most beautiful words in the English language are *summer evening*. For many of us, especially during the week, our time to relax or entertain starts just when the sun is ready to set. There is a bright side to being outdoors after dusk: The heat of the day has faded, the air feels softer, the weeds don't show, and—if you plant an evening garden— you can enjoy luminous and fragrant flowers by moonlight.

Gardens designed for night viewing have been cultivated since medieval times. Moon gardens were quite common during the Victorian age and have been key features in some of this century's most famous gardens—in particular, Sissinghurst Castle, home of the writer Vita Sackville-West. You don't need to own a British estate or employ a full-time crew of gardeners to experience your own bit of twilight magic. Even the most modest planting of white and pale-colored flowers, paired with silver, grey, or blue foliage, will look elegant in daylight and enchanting at night.

Night-blooming flowers, pollinated by moths, wait until late afternoon or twilight to unfold their blossoms and

Evening primrose

release their perfumed fragrances.

Tuck a small bed of such plants beside your patio, in containers on your deck, along the path to your front door, or even in a window box outside your bedroom window. If you choose a spot that gets full sun during the day, which most evening bloomers require, the plants will be in the path of moonbeams at night.

Flowers that open at night tend to be summer bloomers—a real advantage since, for most of the country, that's when it's actually warm enough to sit outside after dark. Of course, you don't have to include

only night-blooming flowers—any plant with grayish silver foliage or with pale-colored blossoms that remain open after dark will look lovely in moonlight.

LIGHTS FOR THE NIGHT GARDEN

Keep in mind when planning your evening garden that you'll need a source of illumination for moonless nights. A few well-placed luminaries, tiki torches, or lanterns will provide the most romantic light. Use an insect-repelling citronella candle or torch, and your lighting can serve two functions at the same time.

A more permanent solution is to install a landscape lighting system. These are now widely available and affordable, and many are simple enough to be installed by the homeowner. If you do choose to use electric lights in your garden, use low-wattage bulbs to create the effect of soft moonlight. Glaring lights will take away from the magical effect of the pale flowers and will also attract bothersome insects.

Play around and have fun when placing the lights in your evening garden. Lights perched in the branches of trees can create the effect of moonlight, while spot lighting best accents a particular plant or small bed. Diffused lighting (bulbs covered with frosted material) gives an appropriate level of light for viewing night-blooming flowers, and the effects of shadowing (positioning a light so the shadow of a plant is cast upon a flat surface) can be stunning.

WATER IN THE NIGHT GARDEN

No night garden is complete without at least a bit of water. The smallest tub of water, if strategically placed, will mirror the moon, while the simplest fountain will provide soothing night music. Artificial waterfalls look lovely (and often more natural) by moonlight, and a small pond will encourage frogs to stop by to serenade you.

Water will allow you to grow even more night-blooming plants. Imagine sipping a cool drink on your terrace as exotic water lilies in a nearby pond open slowly and release their heady perfume. (Many tropical lilies of the genus *Nymphaea* bloom at night.) White irises, white turtleheads, and light-colored grasses are all plants that look lovely at the water's edge at night. (See pages 36 through 39 for more information on backyard water features.)

MOTHS

Viewing the moth (plain-Jane cousin of the elegant butterfly) with pity or scorn is easy. We plant entire gardens with dazzling, bright blooms to lure butterflies to our yards, but we mine our closets with chemicals to keep moths from snacking on our winter woolens.

In truth, the moth, which has 13 times as many species as the butterfly (its fellow member of the order Lepidoptera), is a pretty impressive insect. Butterflies must feed on erect, brightly colored flowers with clearly marked centers that are open in the daylight. But the moth comes equipped with complex, light-gathering eyes; antennae that provide both bal-

ance and a highly developed sense of smell; and a *proboscis* (or tongue) up to six inches long. All these features allow the moth to gather nectar from fragrant flowers that open at night and hide their sustenance in deep, tubelike blossoms.

Planting even one or two evening-blooming flowers will encourage moths to visit your backyard. Evening primroses and honeysuckles are favored by a species commonly called "hawk" or "sphinx" moths. Strong fliers with rapid wingbeats (some can fly up to 30 miles an hour), these moths are often mistaken for hummingbirds because they feed by hovering in front of flowers while sipping nectar through their long proboscises.

Families

Family backyards aren't always picture perfect. Their garden beds may contain a few weeds, their lawns may boast badminton sets instead of elegant koi ponds, and their sunflowers may outnumber their exotic plants. Nevertheless, these backyards can be places where the entire family relaxes and plays.

You'll grow your flowers in beds you've protected from cavorting children, while your children play in specially designed areas. Songbirds will nest comfortably in houses that you've provided for them, and even the family pets will be welcome outdoors—once you've learned how to protect your plants (and the birds) from them.

As your yard becomes a more inviting place, you'll find your children leaving the T.V. behind to play in treehouses, soar on swings, or draw pictures in their garden journals—perhaps of the monarch butterflies that you've lured to your butterfly garden. Or maybe they'll be trying out their trowels in the first garden they've so proudly planted. And you may or may not be pulling those weeds. After all, backyards—like families—aren't meant to be perfect: They're meant to be loved and enjoyed.

Designing Yards for Children

secret to designing yards that children will enjoy is to first remember what it was like to be a child.

ROUGH AND TUMBLE

Just as it would make no sense to outfit a child's playroom with precious oriental carpets, fine lace, and fragile china, it would also be foolish to expect children to romp happily in a yard with weak, finely textured grasses; narrow paths; and delicate plants. Kids need to run, jump, skip, and climb outdoors. They need open spaces for games—preferably areas carpeted with tough, resilient grasses. They require sturdy-limbed trees to climb and swing from; and wide, well-marked paths to trample. Children want plenty of sunshine, but they also need adequate shade. They don't care if your yard wins awards from the local gardening club. Overgrown shrubs provide them with secret forts; problem muddy spots become mysterious swamps to muck about in.

SETTING LIMITS

Does this mean you have to give up your dreams of dazzling, well-designed flower beds? No, because children also need boundaries. Just as you might

No matter how perfectly landscaped your yard, to any small child, it's a wild place, filled with crawling, climbing, slithering creatures; leafy secret passages; vast savannahs of grass; towering trees; and dirt (glorious dirt!). What adults see as a weed's bothersome seed head is—to a child—a magical puff ball to blow upon. A branch knocked onto your manicured lawn by a summer storm can become—for a child—

a pen, a sword, a galloping horse, a conductor's baton, or a flying broomstick. And rocks. What makes children so crazy about rocks? Do your children sometimes seem to have more rocks in their indoor collections than could possibly have existed outside?

Gardening and rearing young children have something important in common. They both force us to slow down, to kneel, and to see the world up close through new/old eyes. The teach your children to treat a special room in your house with extra care, so, too, can they learn that certain sections of the yard are ball-, bat-, and frisbee-free zones. Boundaries such as fences and hedges can help reinforce this idea, while simultaneously hiding some of the less attractive aspects of the kids' areas. Keep such borders low enough to let you keep an eye on the children's play, but high enough to serve as visual demarcations.

Limits also need to be set for safety reasons. Teach children never to put plants in their mouths unless you say it is okay (the list to the right names some of the poisonous plants that can be found in backyards).

BUDDING GARDENERS

No matter how fascinating a play area, children may want to do what you're doing—try their hands at gardening. If so, help them start their own small patch of easy-to-grow plants. (You'll find a plan for a child's garden on page 86.) Keep this starter garden small, and site it in a sunny spot close to a water source. Also remember that a kid's garden should be fun. If gardening instills a little horticultural knowledge or encourages a child to taste broccoli, treat these as bonuses, *not* goals.

PLAY THINGS

While children can usually pass many happy hours playing with nothing but plants, dirt, bugs, sticks, and rocks, you'll probably wind up providing them with outdoor play things anyway. Just remember to purchase items that can stand up to both your children's rambunctious play and the elements.

Climbing structures allow children to do all the things you keep trying to get them to stop doing on your furniture indoors. Remember how quickly children grow, though; select structures that are not only safe and well constructed, but that will also continue to be used a few years down the road.

Swings will not only be swung on; they'll probably be twisted tight and spun wildly, stood upon, and hung upside down from. Make sure they're well made and safely attached, and that the ground below them is softly cushioned. Slides should be sturdy. The metal ones can get terribly hot, so plastic is often a better choice.

Most young children love digging in sandboxes; unfortunately, most cats also find them convenient. Get or make one with a lid to keep out both rain and felines.

And don't forget about playhouses. Can you remember how magical it felt to be a child in your own small, private hideaway? Playhouses can range from free and simple (a cardboard box from an appliance store or vines planted to climb a tepee of bamboo poles) to elaborate and quite costly architecturally-designed play palaces.

Yards are places for exploration and discovery, and kids—fascinated by things we overlook or hurry past—treat them that way naturally. Rather than spoiling their fun by telling them that the yard is an educational haven, encourage your budding scientists and poets by providing them with magnifying glasses, field guides, telescopes, star charts, containers for collections, and journals.

10 Poisonous Backyard Plants

- **Angel trumpet**
  Brugmansia arborea

- **Castor bean**
  Ricinus communis

- **Daffodil bulb**
  Narcissus

- **English yew**
  Taxus baccata

- **Foxglove**
  Digitalis purpurea

- **Glory lily bulb**
  Gloriosa superba

- **Jimson weed**
  Datura stamonium

- **Lantana**
  Lantana

- **Lily-of-the-valley**
  Convallaria majalis

- **Oleander**
  Nerium oleander

Making a Garden Journal

A free hour or two and a few supplies are all you need to make this lovely, leather-bound garden journal. Fill its pages with photos and sketches of your garden and family, pressed flowers and leaves, and other garden memories. Once you've learned the stitching technique with which the signatures (or folded paper sheets) are attached to the cover, you'll be able to make as many journals and albums—in as many sizes and shapes—as you like.

MATERIALS & TOOLS

- One 12" x 15" sheet of leather
- Utility knife
- Pencil and ruler
- Awl or sharp nail
- Large needle
- 4½ yards of waxed linen thread or dental floss
- 31 sheets of 11" x 14" paper (90 lb. weight)
- Five 4" x 5" pieces of colorful fabric
- Small rock

Instructions

1 Using a utility knife—and the photo as a guide—cut out a 1½" x 3" window in the center of the leather sheet.

2 To make the first signature, stack three sheets of paper on

top of each other and fold the stack in half to make six 7" x 11" pages. Repeat to make nine more signatures.

3 Using a pencil and ruler, draw a vertical line down the center of a sheet of 11" x 14" paper, dividing it into two 7" x 11" sections.

4 Spread out the leather cover and center the paper under it. Mark two dots on the paper at the center top and center bottom of the window in the cover. This marked paper will now serve as a hole-punching template.

5 Reopen one of the signatures, and place the template on top of it. Using an awl, punch through each dot in the template to make holes through the open signature. Repeat to punch holes in each of the remaining signatures.

6 Now you'll wrap pieces of fabric over the spines of five signatures. Cut the template down to 4" x 5" and use it as you punch two holes in each piece of fabric to ensure that these holes align with the signature holes.

7 Re-fold a signature, and wrap a piece of fabric around its spine, aligning the holes in the fabric and paper. Repeat with four more signatures. Then stack the folded signatures, alternating those with fabric and those without.

8 Open signature #10 (the top signature in the stack) and position it flat inside the opened cover. Thread the needle and tie a knot on one end. Run the thread in through the signature's top hole and out through the window in the cover. Bring the thread over the top of the spine, back through the same top hole, and out again through the window.

9 Refold signature #10 inside the open cover. (These pages will be in the back of the journal.) Open signature #9 (the next from the stack) and place it inside the cover, on top of signature #10. Holding the journal in one hand, turn it over so the cover faces up and pass the thread back down through the window and through the top hole in signature #9. Turn the journal cover side down. The thread should be coming up from the top hole of signature #9.

10 Bring the thread up over the spine and turn the journal cover side up. You'll see a small horizontal stitch at the top of the window. Pass the thread down under that stitch, pull it up toward the top of the journal, and turn the journal so the cover faces down.

11 Refold signature #9 to close it, open signature #8, and place it inside the cover. Turn the journal so the cover faces up, and pass the thread back down through the window, into the top hole in signature #8. Turn the journal cover side down. The thread should be coming up through the top hole of signature #8.

12 Bring the thread up over the spine and turn the journal so the cover faces up. Bring the thread down under the next small horizontal stitch, pull it up slightly to tighten it, and turn the journal cover side down.

13 Continue adding signatures in this way until the tops of all the signatures are stitched. After bringing the thread under the last horizontal stitch, pass it through the window and back through the top hole in signature #1.

14 Bring the thread down through the bottom hole of signature #1 and out through the window. Bring the thread down the outside of the spine and back around to the inside of signature #1. Then pass the needle back through the bottom hole again and out through the window.

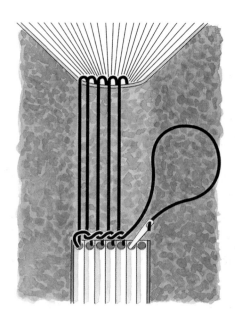

15 Refold signature #1 and open signature #2. Bring the thread through the window and back through the bottom hole in signature #2. Repeat the same stitching technique as you used for the top holes, using the same butterfly stitch to secure each signature.

16 After stitching the last signature, feed the needle back through the window and into the bottom hole of signature #10. Then run the thread underneath the top stitch inside the signature and knot the thread to it. Trim the remaining thread.

17 To make the place marker, wrap a small rock with thread, leaving two long, loose thread ends. Bring the loose thread ends together and tie them to one of the signature stitches on the journal's spine.

Backyards for Birds and Butterflies

Entire families, from toddlers to grandparents, will enjoy a yard where birds sing from the tree branches (or perhaps even raise a brood), and butterflies flutter from flower to flower. With just a bit of planning and planting, you can easily turn your backyard into a beautiful sanctuary for birds and butterflies.

SHELTER FOR BIRDS

From a bird's-eye-view, your backyard is appealing if it offers a place to hide, a place to escape harsh weather, and a place to nest, feed, and drink. The more of these requirements you can fulfill for a particular type of bird, the

more likely that species will be to reward you with a visit or perhaps a long-term stay.

Birds need to be able to hide from predators. Many will look for cover in thorny shrubs, such as hollies, rhododendrons, and roses. Birds that tend to remain low to the ground will seek cover in berry thickets or even ivy.

Evergreen trees will attract birds because they provide both cover from predators and shelter from the cold, wind, rain, and hot sun. Plant pines, firs, hemlocks, or junipers, and you'll soon see a rise in your bird population.

To encourage birds to nest and raise their young in your yard, make

sure you provide a variety of plants: grasses, thickets, shrubs, and taller trees. Birds will be especially attracted to these if they're located in a quiet part of your property. Hollies, dogwoods, hemlocks, and oaks are all trees that encourage nesting.

FOOD AND WATER FOR BIRDS

A variety of birds can coexist in one place because they feed (as well as nest) in separate niches in that area. Just as with nesting, diversity is the key to planting a backyard bird banquet. By including tall, medium, and low-growing food plants for birds, you'll ensure that many different birds will feed in your yard.

It's also important to choose a mix of plants that will produce food throughout the year. Maples offer a feast of seeds in the spring, dogwoods produce berries in the summer, grasses set seed in autumn, and winterberries (as their name indicates) provide berries in winter. Other plants that produce seeds for birds include spider flowers, cornflowers, cosmos, and snapdragons.

Growing native plants is a great way to attract birds. To entice a specific type of bird, refer to a field guide (or contact a local conservation group) to find out what plants that bird feeds on. A bird's beak will usually provide some clues to its diet. Hummingbirds use their long thin beaks to probe nectar from funnel-shaped flowers, while woodpeckers' strong, sharp beaks puncture trees to find insects. And speaking of insects, remember that when you use pesticides to kill off all the bugs in your garden, you'll be eliminating an important food source for many birds.

The birds dining in your yard will also need fresh, clean water. If you already have a small pond or stream, you're set; otherwise, a bird bath should suffice. Because different birds are happiest with different water depths (chickadees and goldfinches like fairly shallow water, while robins and blue jays prefer deeper water), consider adding a couple of small rocks to your bird bath.

A wet bird is hindered in its ability to fly and escape enemies. Therefore, it's important to position your bird bath in an area open enough that cats can't launch surprise attacks, yet close enough to shrubs or trees that birds can wing it to cover quickly.

BUTTERFLIES

As luck would have it, most of the plants that attract butterflies are plants we humans find attractive, too. Your butterfly garden can be one of the most colorful, sunny spots in your yard. Butterflies, like other insects, are cold-blooded; in order to fly, they need the sun to warm them. Most of the plants that butterflies rely on are also sun-lovers. Butterflies frequent gardens with large splashes of color, as colors help them find the nectar they feed on. As you plant a butterfly garden, group together flowers with similar colors instead of scattering them.

Try to have butterfly-friendly plants blooming continuously from spring through fall. For instance, you might plant lilac for spring blooms, butterfly bush for the summer, and chrysanthemum for autumn. The list of plants that attract butterflies is so extensive (sunflowers, zinnias, heliotrope, lantana, and verbena are but a small sample) that you'll easily find flowers to suit your site conditions and landscape plans.

Along with providing the flowers that offer nectar for adult butterflies,

your garden should also contain the plants that caterpillars feed upon. Different species of butterflies choose different plants as the host plants upon which to lay their eggs. Black swallowtails lay their eggs on parsley, while monarchs use milkweed as a host.

Along with food, butterflies will need a water source. A shallow dish sunk into the ground and filled with water can serve this purpose. Add a few very small rocks or a cluster of pebbles to provide landing pads.

Flat rocks can serve another purpose in your garden if you set them in spots that receive a lot of light. Butterflies like to sunbathe on them and warm themselves up before flying.

Bird-Watching

Bird-watching, believe it or not, is one of the most popular hobbies in the world. More than one-third of the population of the United States feeds birds, and bird-watching is the fastest-growing outdoor activity in the country. Why? Perhaps because birds are a delightful source of year-round entertainment and can be found wherever food and water are available to them—including in the smallest of backyards.

BIRDING BASICS

If you're new to bird-watching, you'll want to pick up a good bird-identification book. The best of these are organized so you can quickly identify birds by one or more categories: their shapes, colors, markings, habitats, and niches. (While different bird species often live in the same habitat, each does best in a particular niche of that habitat—on the forest floor or high in the treetops, for example.)

Most bird-watchers keep lists of their sightings. If you're providing food at a feeder, your list is bound to grow as your food supply becomes better known to all the different birds in the area. The entire family can have fun adding new birds to the list. You could also keep a more detailed

Summer tanager

notebook in which you record the date, weather conditions, activities, and exact locations of birds you spot in your yard.

WHEN TO WATCH BIRDS

Dawn and dusk—when birds are most active—are the best times of day for bird-watching. Good bird-watching opportunities exist year-round and in almost any location. In the leafless woods and yards of winter, birds are easier to see. When spring arrives, large numbers of birds migrate north, singing loudly to establish their breeding territories and flaunting bright plumage to attract mates. By midsummer, some birds begin their winter migration, and by the fall, these flocks have swelled with new offspring.

BIRD-WATCHING TIPS AND ETHICS

Remember, as an appreciative and caring audience, your role is to be as unobtrusive as possible while bird-watching. Never flush birds out of hiding or disturb their nesting sites by approaching them too closely. Birds are keenly aware of the presence of humans, so the less visible and audible you are, the more birds you're likely to see. Either situate yourself in a comfortable, stationary spot, or—if you'd rather walk through your property—move in as nonthreatening a way as possible (as carefully and quietly as a cat).

If you're in the company of friends, avoid talking loudly. And when you take a break to go indoors, don't dash—and don't let the door slam behind you. Sudden movements, such as pointing or grabbing for your binoculars, will drive birds away. While you probably won't want to turn your patio table on its side and use it as camouflage, it will help to stay as hidden as possible.

Keep an eye on the weather, too. Strong winds can tire migrating birds, causing them to land in unexpected places. When the weather lightens up, they resume their flight. Low-pressure zones and cold fronts drive migrating birds ahead of them.

To bring an elusive bird into view, try making a "ch-ch-ch-ch-ch-ch" sound; some birds will respond by flying closer and answering with their own chatter. It's important to stop this tactic as soon as you glimpse the bird, however, as this particular sound can cause birds undue stress.

Playing tapes of bird calls has a similar effect, but again, play the tape only briefly; tapes played for long periods of time may disrupt nesting and cause other problems. (For these reasons, playing tapes has been banned in some refuges.)

BIRDS OF A FEATHER

One of the fastest ways to learn about birding is to join one of the many organizations that sponsor outings and tours. Your local library or conservation organizations can put you in touch with a group of birders in your area.

Eastern bluebird

BEGINNING BIRD-WATCHER'S TOOL KIT

Field Guide. Buy an up-to-date field guide to birds. A little practice using it will help you narrow your search when you're trying to identify a bird. If you're a beginner, start with a field guide that covers only the birds in your region.

Binoculars. Binoculars are numbered to indicate their magnification power and their brightness. The 7 in binoculars that are 7 x 40, for example, indicates that the viewed object will be magnified 7 times, while the number 40 represents the

diameter (in millimeters) of the front lenses. The wider the front lenses, the brighter the object—and the heavier the binoculars. The binoculars you select should be between 7x and 10x.

Clothing. If you're watching birds during the winter, be sure to wear warm clothing—sitting still on a porch or patio in the cold can be agonizing unless you're dressed properly! To attract hummingbirds during the summer, wear red! A hat will offer protection in any kind of weather.

Spotting Scopes. Best for long-range viewing of nesting birds, feeder birds, or shore birds, spotting scopes are most useful in the 25x to 30x range and come in two eyepiece styles: one aligned with the barrel, and the other elevated at a 45-degree angle.

Pack. For bird-watching expeditions out of your yard, a day pack will keep your hands free while protecting your gear from the elements. A birding vest, with pockets tailored to hold a field guide and binoculars, will also come in handy.

A Plan for a Child's First Garden

For a child, planting a garden like the one shown below can be a tremendously exciting experience. First, there's the chance to get as dirty as you like while you dig up the garden bed. Then there's getting to buy all those colorful seed packets and baby plants from the nursery. Once they're tucked into their new home, there's the joy of spotting the first tip of an emerging green shoot, and the wonderful taste of that first ripe strawberry. Of course, a garden is an education in itself—a class in patience ("When will those seeds finally sprout?"); in decision-making ("What kind of flowers should I plant?"); in gardening science ("You mean that dead leaves are sort of like food for the food I'm growing?"); and in paying attention ("Whoops! That sunflower looks thirsty! I'd better start remembering to water it.").

A PEPPERMINT

Mentha x piperita

Hardiness zones 3–7

12 to 36 inches tall

Whorls of lavender flowers in summer; fragrant, green leaves; rich, moist soil; full sun; can be invasive

B BELL PEPPER

Capsicum annuum 'Grossum Group'

Annual

2 to 3 feet tall

Sweet, bell-shaped, green peppers, ripen to yellow, red, or deep purple; matures in 50 to 75 days; fertile, evenly moist, well-drained soil; full sun

C PLUM TOMATO

Lycopersicon esculentum 'Roma'

Annual

4 to 10 feet tall

Plum-shaped fruits all summer; matures in 70 to 80 days; fertile, evenly moist, well-drained soil; full sun

D ALPINE STRAWBERRY

Fragaria vesca

Hardiness zones 3–7

6 to 10 inches tall

Small white or pink blossoms turn into small, flavorful fruits early summer to frost; starts very slowly from seed (buy plants); fertile, well-drained soil; full sun

E SNAPDRAGON

Antirrhinum majus

Hardiness zones 5–9

6 to 36 inches tall

Tubular, double-lipped flowers in many colors all summer; lance-shaped, deep green leaves; average to rich, well-drained soil; full sun

F SWEET POTATO VINE

Ipomoea batatas 'Blackie'

Hardiness zones 9–11

up to 20 feet tall

Tender perennial vine with large, purple-black leaves; grown as ornamental for foliage; well-drained soil; full sun

G GLOBE AMARANTH

Gomphrena globosa

Annual

12 to 24 inches tall

Cloverlike flowers in many colors summer to frost; oblong, hairy, mid-green leaves; moderately fertile, well-drained soil; full sun; flowers dry well

H SCARLET RUNNER BEAN

Phaseolus coccineus

Annual

6 to 10 feet tall

Bright scarlet, pea-like flowers cover vine early to midsummer, then 4- to 12-inch pods with seeds speckled black and red; dark green leaves with three leaflets; moist, well-drained soil; full sun; both flowers and seeds are edible

I SUNFLOWER

Helianthus annuus

Hardiness zones 4–9

2 to 10 feet tall

Large, yellow, daisylike flowers with yellow, brown, or purple disk florets; large, heart-shaped mid- to dark green leaves; moderately fertile, moist, well-drained soil; full sun; seeds are edible

Pets in the Garden

Is it possible to have both a wonderfully landscaped backyard and happy pets? The answer, as evidenced by countless pet-loving gardeners across the country, is a resounding *yes!* Just as children and gardens can peacefully coexist, so, too, can pets and plants. Gardening does, however, pose special challenges for pet owners and their pets. Toxic plants and poisons and even wildlife can be dangerous to your pets, and, without training, your animal companions may decide your garden beds make perfect litter boxes. Your dog will wag its tail with delight at the digging pits you've so thoughtfully cultivated, and your cat may think it most kind of you to be luring those birds to the yard with feeders. But with a little care and planning you can keep both your pets and your garden safe.

KEEPING YOUR GARDEN SAFE

For some cats, a garden is one grand litter box. Surprising cats with a quick squirt of water from a spray bottle can sometimes discourage such unwanted behavior. For particularly willful cats, consider laying chicken wire on the soil before planting, or purchase a pet-deterrent spray or powder from a pet store. (Check the safety of such products before using them near edible plants.) Never use soiled litter as a fertilizer; it's not only a health hazard, but it will also attract other cats to your yard.

The main challenge posed by dogs in the garden is digging. Dogs dig for a variety of reasons. Sometimes they are hunting rodents beneath the ground; sometimes they're creating a "den" (remember dogs are descendants of wolves). But dogs also dig for the sheer joy of it—digging is fun! If your dog digs trenches, it's probably hunting moles or other small rodents. Taking steps to eliminate this prey from your yard will help curb this activity. If your dog seems to be digging holes and then lying in them, make sure you are providing shelter that is cool in summer and warm in winter. Dogs that dig as a recreational sport need to be given plenty of exercise and attention. Try teaching your pet the command "No digging," filling holes with things the dog won't enjoy pouncing on (chicken wire and water balloons work well), or providing a doggie sandbox (burying your dog's toys and treats there will encourage its use).

Cats and dogs often eat grass, sometimes to add nutrients to their diets and more often to provide a stomach irritant that will help them eliminate something they've ingested. To discourage this behavior, try feeding them other vegetables. Raw broccoli, cauliflower, and carrots are good choices, but avoid onions and potatoes. Alternatively, you could grow a container of grass just for your pet on your patio or even indoors.

KEEPING PETS SAFE

If you notice your pet eating vegetation other than grass, don't assume it's harmless. Various parts of many common plants, such as morning glories, daffodils, rhododendrons, azaleas, rhubarb, and tomato plants, can be toxic. If your pet seems disoriented, is salivating excessively, or has an upset stomach after eating a plant, take the animal to

a vet, and bring along a sample of anything you think your pet may have ingested. Do not allow your pets onto lawns that have been recently treated with fertilizers or pesticides. Take special care whenever you apply insecticides, weed killers, and fertilizers.

KEEPING WILDLIFE SAFE

Domestic animals and wild animals rarely coexist peacefully without human intervention. Remember, your cat is

not a natural part of your backyard ecosystem. Install bird feeders at least five feet above ground level and in an area clear of brush. Try to keep birdseed off the ground, too, as fallen seed makes birds easier prey for cats, and ingesting birdseed can be harmful to your pets. Try using a suet feeder instead of a seed feeder or surrounding your seed feeder with chicken wire. Unfortunately, bell collars on cats are probably less effective than you think. Cats stalk slowly and then pounce. By the time a bird hears the bell, it's often too late.

Finally, don't overlook your pets when planting your garden. Easy-to-grow catnip and valerian root are both harmless kitty intoxicants. Just make sure you start the seedlings someplace safe from your cat! And unless you want your cat to play in a garden bed, plant catnip away from it. Because catnip spreads easily, it's best to keep it in a pot, buried to the rim. Once the plant is mature, just pinch off the leaves and buds for your cat to play with, or dry and store them for a special treat. If you have birds, consider growing your own seed. Rabbits, hamsters, and gerbils will appreciate all sorts of treats from your garden.

Health & History

Imagining your backyard garden as a florist's shop or as a grocery store stocked with fresh produce is easy. Just picture yourself arranging a bouquet of fresh-cut flowers or plucking a sun-warmed tomato from the vine. But what if one corner of your garden were a pharmacy offering free prescriptions for good health? And another boasted a botanical museum—filled with descendants of centuries-old plants? And yet another included a collection of wild-flowers and native plants?

While you may not want to learn the fine points of herbal medicine, there's no reason you can't turn to your own backyard for the stimulating scent of lavender or a soothing cup of chamomile tea. And why not bring touches of history and local inter-est to your yard by setting out a few heir-loom and native plants? Wildflowers and native plants provide almost maintenance-free pleasure all season long. Heirloom flowers and vegetables—grown from seed that's been carefully harvested and passed along through the centuries—offer the rich flavors, vivid colors, and perfumed scents that our ancestors enjoyed.

Heirloom Gardening

Any seed holds an almost magical potential, but if it is an heirloom seed, then it also holds a vast store of history. Passed down from generation to generation of gardeners, heirloom seeds provide a rare opportunity to see and taste and smell the world as our ancestors did—long before technology began genetically altering the food and flowers we grow.

HEIRLOOM AND HYBRID PLANTS

Most of the fruits and vegetables offered in our supermarkets' produce sections (and most of the seeds offered by large commercial seed companies) are hybrids. They come from plants that have been genetically engineered to produce fruits and vegetables that ripen uniformly, can be mechanically harvested, have tough skins that will survive shipping, and have a long shelf life.

Heirloom plants, on the other hand, are plants that have been passed (usually by seed) from gardener to gardener for years—sometimes even centuries. Some heirlooms, such as 'Pink Hopi' corn, are natives, but others came to this country as seeds in the pockets of immigrants, who brought their favorite varieties from their homelands.

Hollyhock

One reason these antique plants have endured is that they are open-pollinated, that is, they reproduce from seed and the resultant plants come back true to type. Hybrid plants (the offspring of a cross between two parent varieties that are genetically different) produce seed that either won't grow or that grow into plants that revert back to one of the parent plants rather than remaining true to type.

THE VALUE OF HEIRLOOM PLANTS

In the last several years, interest in heirlooms has blossomed as more and more gardeners discover the rewards of growing purple-skinned carrots and 15-pound cabbages or the same flowers that decorated their grandmothers' backyards. Their appeal is not solely historic. Heirlooms often boast richer flavors and fragrance than hybrids. Because of this, restaurants are beginning to serve dishes that feature heirlooms,

Great blue lobelia

and antique roses and other heirloom flowers are making a comeback.

Many advocates of heirlooms are also worried about the fact that we have lost so many of the food plants that were once available in this country. It's estimated that 75 percent of the native food plants growing when Columbus first set foot on our soil are now gone forever. And today we have only a tiny fraction of the plant varieties cultivated 100 years ago.

The value of diversity in plant varieties isn't just a matter of having a wide range of tomatoes to choose from when we make a dinner salad. Lack of genetic diversity can have serious repercussions. Because most of the potatoes grown in Ireland during the 1840s were of only one variety, a fungus was able to spread and wipe out the entire crop. More than one million people died in the resulting famine.

ACQUIRING AND GROWING HEIRLOOM PLANTS

A network of seed collectors all over the country is now intent on preserving the cultural heritage and diversity of our plants. Probably the largest single resource accessible to enthusiasts is the Seed Savers Exchange, a non-profit organization with its own 170-acre farm and seed bank, in Iowa. More and more of these seed exchanges are springing up across the country (some can be found listed in magazines; many are listed on the internet).

TOMATOES: 'Yellow Pear,' 'Red Pear,' 'Yellow Perfection,' 'Riesenstraube,' and 'Slava'

Seed companies specializing in or including heirloom seed in their offerings are also on the rise.

If you'd like to try your hand at growing a few living antiques—perhaps a lobelia that's been gracing gardens since the fifteenth century or a yellow pear tomato—keep in mind that heirloom seeds are sometimes slow to germinate. In fact, some will shoot up even after you've given them up for dead.

SAVING HEIRLOOM SEEDS

After you've enjoyed your heirloom plants' sumptuous flavors or perfumed blossoms, you'll want to save some seed for next year's crop or for a gardening friend. Complete information on saving seeds from different plants is available from many seed exchanges, but the process is usually quite simple.

One trick is to collect seeds only from plants that are isolated from other varieties; the seeds of different varieties will hybridize if the plants are grown too close together. Another is to let the seed grow to maturity, which in many instances means allowing the vegetable or flower to mature long past the time you would normally harvest it. The seeds are then separated from the fruit or vegetable, and if they're moist, are sometimes sun-dried for a brief period of time. Then they're stored in a cool, dry place (often the refrigerator) until the next growing season.

By saving heirloom seeds, you'll become one more link in the valuable chain that helps us protect and preserve some of our most valuable inheritances.

Passalong and Commemorative Plants

Hens and chickens

Peony

As much as we gardeners are a competitive bunch (peeking over the neighbors' fences to see if their tulips will open before ours this spring), we are also a generous group. Folks who truly love plants are happy to spread the wealth; after all, flower beds grow crowded, and who could bear to toss an old friend onto the compost heap?

PASSALONGS

In their book, *Passalong Plants,* Steven Bender and Felder Rushing define passalongs as plants that are easy to propagate yet hard to find commercially. Just as heirloom plants have survived despite the big nurseries' and seed companies' push for hybrids, passa-

long plants have also endured, thanks to gardeners with generous hearts (and crowded flower beds). Even plants that are readily available from nurseries can be fun to pass along—just be sure they are easily propagated.

Typically, plants get passed along in the most informal of manners. You express admiration for a certain perennial, and the proud gardener digs up a clump with a few good roots and says, "Here, have some." Or your daylilies need dividing so you offer the extras to your neighbor (who reminds you that she gave them to you in the first place when she thinned her own overgrown clump three years ago). Sometimes local garden clubs hold plant swaps (each person comes with a plant

to give away and leaves with a new one). Gardeners interested in preserving and sharing heirloom or other specialty seeds have begun organizing groups, and more and more seed exchanges are taking place in magazines and on the internet.

These humble plants have much to recommend them. Not only are they easy to propagate from seed, cuttings, or division; they also tend to be self-sufficient. While catalogs from the other side of the country offer all sorts of horticultural temptations, paying close attention to what grows for your

Trumpet vine

neighbors is a golden rule of gardening. If the eighty-year-old woman next door has a peony she remembers playing beside as a child, you know it's a plant with staying power that likes your climate.

In fact, the local climate will influence just which plants are most commonly passed along in your region. Hens and chickens (the succulent you might remember from your grandmother's rock garden); spider flower (a tall, reseeding annual with large, whiskery flower heads); and money plant (a biennial with flat, translucent seedpods that resemble coins) are just three examples of the hundreds of plants that have made their way into countless yards by being passed over the back fence from gardener to gardener.

COMMEMORATIVE PLANTS

Cut flowers have long been used to mark special occasions, but living plants can serve as gifts or memorials that only become more meaningful with the passage of time. Plant a sapling to celebrate your child's birth, and his or her grandchildren may one day swing from its branches. Present newlyweds with a fragrant shrub in June and it will flower for countless anniversaries to come. Helping to tend to a small shrub planted in remembrance of a pet that's passed away can let children express their grief while instilling respect for the natural cycles of life.

Commemorative plants should be easy to care for and long-lived. Daylilies, bearded iris, peonies, and Asiatic lilies are examples of flowering plants that will last for many years (and in some cases multiply) in the right conditions. Weeping cherry or dogwood trees will flower each spring for years to come, while dwarf evergreens will brighten the winter landscape without ever growing too tall.

Special care should be taken when giving a plant as a gift. The recipient's local climate and specific soil and sun conditions should be taken into account. For plants as substantial as a shrub or tree, it is best to ask for personal preferences. Purchase healthy, disease- and insect-free plants, and make sure you include instructions for planting and care.

10 Passalong Plants

- **Cosmos**
  Cosmos bipinnatus

- **Corn poppy**
  Papaver rhoeas

- **Hens and chickens**
  Sempervivum

- **Hollyhock**
  Alcea rosea

- **Honesty**
  Lunaria annua

- **Lamb's-ears**
  Stachys byzantina

- **Larkspur**
  Consolida ajacis

- **Rose campion**
  Lychnis coronaria

- **Spider flower**
  Cleome hassleriana

- **Trumpet vine**
  Campsis radicans

Spider flower

Native Species and Wildflowers

Many gardeners have discovered a series of valuable secrets right before their eyes: Native plants (plants indigenous to the areas in which they grow) thrive in local backyards, attract native wildlife, are relatively pest-free, typically require less water than non-native plants, and boast a beauty all their own.

Native plants are sometimes referred to as wildflowers, but not all wildflowers originated where they now grow. Wildflowers are simply plants that have naturalized (or gone wild); one of their benefits is that they grow easily with little or no care. The only problem is when a non-native wildflower grows too well. Then it can become invasive and threaten native plants and wildlife.

Claret-cup cactus

Jack-in-the-pulpit

GARDEN HISTORY

Traditionally, gardens in the United States were (and often still are) re-creations of the homeland gardens of the immigrants who settled here. While the plants in these gardens grow well in their countries of origin, they're sometimes not suited to their new homes. The green, manicured lawns so common in the United States, for example, originated in England, where ample rainfall keeps lawns lush. Maintaining lawns as luxurious in the desert regions of the southwestern United States requires massive amounts of water and fertilizer. Enlightened desert gardeners have turned instead to the beauty of native plants such as blue gamma, native buffalo grass, prickly poppy, and claret-cup cactus, to name just a few—all plants that are perfectly suited to their desert environments, both in their growth habits and in their appearance.

FINDING NATIVE PLANTS AND WILDFLOWERS

To locate native plants and wildflowers adapted to your region, contact your local Cooperative Extension Service or a wildflower society. A growing number of nurseries specialize in native plants, and even those that don't will frequently offer a few native species. Botanical gardens are also good sources. When purchasing a native plant, find out where it came from by looking for the term "nursery propagated" (not "nursery grown") in the nursery catalog or on the plant label. Buying a nursery-propagated plant ensures that the plant wasn't simply removed from its natural habitat—a practice that endangers plant communities. (In North America, there are hundreds of endangered species, all threatened by reckless collecting.) Many wildflowers are easily propagated from seed, which more and more seed companies are offering, often as a mix of various wildflowers.

One of the best ways to decide which native plants or wildflowers you'd like to try in your garden is to observe what's growing in the wild or along roadsides. Which of these plant combinations pleases your eye? North America is particularly rich in its variety of native plants, and there are countless ones to choose from, whether you live in a desert or tropical environment.

LANDSCAPING

In natural areas, different plant species grow together in a community. These, in turn, create the perfect environment for other types of plants. To emulate this rich harmony in your own garden, plant many individuals of a given species and then blend in at least one other compatible type of plant.

When gardening with native species, it's often more appropriate to enhance the natural lay of your land than it is

to force a level surface by creating a flat bed as you might for non-native flowers. If you live in a desert region, you might want to shape the uneven surface of your yard into a creek bed— a desert arroyo—which can serve as a walkway when dry and an irrigation canal for plants when it carries water from a thunderstorm.

If you live in the eastern woodlands and have a perpetually wet spot in your yard, try planting a combination of cinnamon fern, cardinal flower, and bee balm. Then sit back and enjoy the hummingbirds that will seek out the brilliant cardinal flowers.

If your yard is too small for much gardening, plant natives in containers. Ageratum, trumpet honeysuckle, Christmas fern, celandine poppy, and blueberry will all do well in small spaces.

AN INSTANT NATURAL AREA

An easy way to start a wildflower and native plant garden is to stop mowing an area of your yard. Let the grass grow, and it will gradually create an environment for pioneer plants that are planted by birds, small animals, and the wind. Over time, the new plants will shade out the grass. To speed the process along, you can pull the grass and introduce more wildflowers and native plants. But remember, these gardens will never be perfectly landscaped, tidy beds. The emphasis here is on "wild."

Bitterweed

The Healing Garden

Lavender

St. John's wort

I n every culture, throughout the centuries, the knowledge of herbal remedies has been recorded and passed down by healers and herb gatherers. Native Americans, for example, honored certain indigenous plants as valued remedies for common complaints, and early immigrants to the New World cultivated non-native healing plants from the carefully preserved seeds they brought with them. Today, many active ingredients in pharmaceutical preparations are plant-based, and medicinal uses for new plants are still being discovered.

Even in the tiniest suburban backyard, a medicinal garden can add a sense of the mystery and magic of traditional healing gardens of the past. One caution, however: Plants are powerful. Never ingest one unless you know exactly what it is and exactly what effects it will have! If you're interested in growing and using medicinal herbs, a variety of helpful books is available.

MEDICINE WHEEL DESIGN

One of the most common medicinal garden designs is the traditional medicine wheel, in which herbs are planted in wedges around a center-point. If you'd like to try your hand at designing a wheel of your own, you may find the following suggestions helpful:

Plant the center of the wheel with the lovely *Echinacea* (or purple cone-flower), which is believed to have cleansing and purifying qualities. Then surround the circle with a hedge of lavender, which will add its uplifting fragrance, as well as headache-soothing blossoms. Try planting a few rosemary shrubs with the lavender; they're reputed to dispel melancholy.

A wedge of the apple-scented, daisylike flowers of chamomile and a spot of lemon balm will both yield calming teas. Peppermint will aid digestion, and sage—when it's transformed into a gargle—will soothe sore throats.

Yarrow is valued for its antiseptic and wound-healing qualities; and bee balm, with its scarlet blossoms, can relieve nausea. Calendula will soothe irritated skin, and St. John's wort will calm the nerves.

WILD MEDICINAL GARDEN

If your gardening style is informal, just set aside a wild area of your yard, mow a path through the center, and wait to see what herbal allies will emerge. Herbs as common as dandelion, chicory, curly dock, the bold burdock with its deep root, and the downy-leafed mullein with its tall stalks of golden flowers are all powerful plant remedies. Early in spring, notice the blue violets (which are high in vitamin C) and the creeping, starlike flowers of chickweed. Plantain leaves, bright red clover blossoms,

Purple coneflower

purslane, self heal, wild strawberry, and blessed thistle are all medicinal herbs. If you take along a good reference book to help you identify these common allies and companionable healers, each excursion into the wild spaces of your backyard can become an adventure of discovery and joy.

ONE-OF-A-KIND MEDICINAL GARDENS

The only real limits to the way in which you design a medicinal herb garden should be the amount of space you have, the time available to you for garden care

Rosemary

and maintenance—and a healthy concern for safety.

People who believe that herbs release their healing properties through their colors and scents will often design medicinal gardens for these qualities only. Other gardens have plants selected for their specific medicinal properties. The thousands of herbs known for their healing capacities will provide you with a myriad possibilities for garden designs. And researching the folk wisdom and lore surrounding each of these plants will add another dimension of interest to a wonderful backyard project.

A Medicinal Garden Plan

The plants in this small medicinal garden are among the hundreds that herbalists have recommended through the centuries for complaints ranging from fatigue to headaches and indigestion. (You'll find descriptions of these herbs' uses on page 105.) In recent years, as natural health-care methods have become increasingly popular, easy-to-grow medicinal herbs are appearing in more and more gardens. Even if you don't want to relax with a cup of home-grown lemon balm tea or soothe a sore throat with a sage-tea gargle, you'll find that the plants' flowers and foliage make lovely additions to any garden bed.

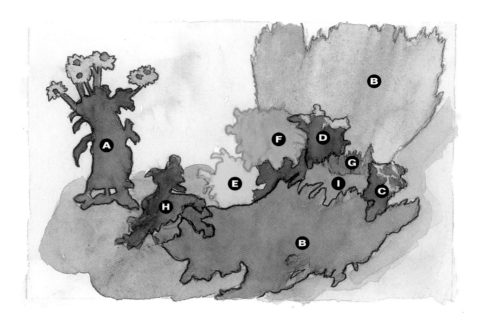

A PURPLE CONEFLOWER
Echinacea purpurea

Hardiness zones 3–9

2 to 4 feet tall

Deep purple to rose to white, drooping petals, with dark brown conical centers midsummer to early fall; lance-shaped, dark green leaves; well-drained loam; full sun to light shade

B ROSEMARY
Rosmarinus

Hardiness zones 8–10

6 inches to 7 feet tall

Tiny pale blue, pink, or lavender flowers mid-spring to early summer; fragrant, needlelike leaves used in cooking; well-drained, alkaline soil; full sun

C ROMAN CHAMOMILE
Chamaemelum nobile

Hardiness zones 6–9

1 to 6 inches tall

Small, white, daisylike flowers with golden centers late spring to early fall; bright green ferny foliage; dry, well-drained soil; full sun to light shade

D CALENDULA
Calendula officinalis

Annual

12 to 24 inches tall

Orange, yellow, or cream, daisylike flowers all summer; oval, deep green leaves; poor to average, well-drained soil; full sun

E GOLDEN SAGE
Salvia officinalis 'Aurea'

Hardiness zones 4–8

1 to 2 feet tall

Small spikes of lavender blue flowers in early summer; fragrant, variegated yellow and green leaves used in cooking; well-drained soil; full sun

F BASIL
Ocimum basilicum

Annual

1 to 2 feet tall

Small, white, tubular flowers midsummer to frost; fragrant, green or purple leaves used in cooking; rich, moist, well-drained soil; full sun

G LAVENDER
Lavandula angustifolia

Hardiness zones 5–10

1 to 4 feet tall

Fragrant, lavender flower spikes late spring to summer; fragrant, woolly, gray-green foliage; well-drained soil; full sun

H LEMON BALM
Melissa officinalis

Hardiness zones 3–7

2 to 4 feet tall

Spikes of yellow or white, tubular flowers in summer; fragrant, wrinkled, light green leaves; well-drained soil; full sun

I PARSLEY
Petroselinum crispum

Annual

up to 32 inches tall

Crinkled bright green to dark green leaves used in cooking; fertile, moist, well-drained soil; full sun

Making Tinctures and Decoctions

In order to render herbs useful as medicinals, various plant parts are included in tinctures, decoctions, infusions, syrups, salves, and poultices. The method of preparation depends on the plant, the part used, and the results sought.

Two recipes are provided here: one for a tincture and one for a decoction. A tincture is a water- or alcohol-based solution that contains an extraction of the essential active ingredients of the plant or plants. Alcohol-based tinctures are usually mixed in a ratio of one part finely-cut herb to five parts 60- to 70-proof brandy, vodka, or gin. A decoction is made by simmering plant parts (often roots or seeds) in water.

Echinacea Tincture

Many health-food stores carry versions of this simple tincture, which has become very popular as a method for battling viruses. Echinacea is also thought to help promote proper digestion and cleanse the blood.

MATERIALS & TOOLS

- Trowel
- Sharp knife
- ½ cup (or 4 ounces by volume) of clean and finely chopped echinacea (*Echinacea purpurea*) rhizome or root
- 1 pint of brandy, vodka, or gin
- 1 quart glass jar with lid
- Dark glass storage bottles with eyedropper lids
- Cheesecloth
- Sieve
- Mixing bowl
- Labels

TIPS

- No matter what herbal preparation you're making, gather your herbs on a sunny morning, after the dew has dried. Fresh herbs usually yield the most vital and effective remedies, but if you don't have access to any, purchase dried herbs at a health-food store.
- Dark glass bottles with dropper lids are available at many health-food stores.
- A safe dosage for this tincture is 15 to 20 drops diluted in water or orange juice, taken three times daily.

INSTRUCTIONS

1 Echinacea is a perennial. Harvest the roots and rhizomes during the autumn, when the flowers and leaves have died back, or in the spring, before the plant begins to grow again. Dig up the roots carefully, removing only as much as you need for your tincture and leaving plenty of undisturbed roots for the next growing season.

2 Clean the root thoroughly under cold running water. Then chop it finely.

3 Place ½ cup of chopped root in a clean glass jar. Add one pint of brandy, gin, or vodka, and cover the jar tightly.

4 Place the sealed jar in a cabinet or dark corner for two weeks, shaking well at least once a day.

5 After two weeks, line a sieve with several layers of cheesecloth, and place the sieve over a mixing bowl. Pour the solution through the sieve, and then pour the strained tincture into dark glass dropper-top bottles.

6 Label each bottle with the tincture name and preparation date, and store the bottles in a cool, dark place. Because the alcohol acts as a preservative, the tinctures will keep for up to two years.

Dandelion Decoction

The common dandelion (*Taraxacum officinale*) is a traditional favorite in many folk remedies for aiding digestion. The medicinal part used in this decoction is the long taproot.

MATERIALS & TOOLS

- Trowel
- Sharp knife
- Enamel or glass saucepan
- Filtered water
- ½ cup of clean, chopped dandelion roots
- Cheesecloth or muslin
- Sieve
- Mixing bowl
- Dark glass jars for storage

TIPS

- Decoctions don't stay fresh for very long, so make only what you'll drink in a few days' time.
- Take one tablespoon of this decoction three times daily. (If you suffer from persistent stomach ailments or from gallstones, do not use the decoction at all; consult your physician instead.)

INSTRUCTIONS

1 Dig the dandelion roots in the fall, after the plants flower, or use whole plants in early spring.

2 Clean the roots thoroughly and then slice them into thin rounds.

3 Place the rounds in a saucepan, and add two pints of filtered water.

4 Bring the water to a boil, turn down the heat, and simmer gently until the liquid has been reduced to one pint.

5 Allow the mixture to cool. Line a sieve with several layers of cheesecloth and place the sieve over a mixing bowl. Pour the decoction through the cheesecloth.

6 Store the strained decoction in a dark glass jar, and keep the jar sealed and refrigerated between uses. Decoctions will stay fresh for only a few days.

Making an Herbal Foot Bath

TIPS

- Any of the following herbs may be used in an herbal footbath: basil (invigorates and deodorizes); bay (relieves aching); bergamot (invigorates and relieves itching); chamomile (soothes irritated skin); horsetail (refreshes); hyssop (relaxes and relieves stiffness); lavender (invigorates and refreshes); lemon balm (invigorates and refreshes); lovage (deodorizes); marjoram (soothes aches); meadowsweet (relaxes); mugwort (eases fatigue and restores flexibility); peppermint (refreshes); rosemary (relieves aching); sage (soothes); thyme (cleanses).
- Decoctions may be stored in the refrigerator for a few days, but they're most effective when fresh.
- Fresh herbs are always more potent than dried ones, but if your garden isn't home to any of the herbs suggested above, visit your local health-food store and purchase dried ones instead.

MATERIALS & TOOLS

- ½ cup of fresh herbs or ¼ cup of dried herbs
- 6 cups of water
- Large enamel or stainless steel saucepan
- Sieve
- Cheesecloth
- Large glass or stainless steel mixing bowl
- 5 teaspoons of sea salt
- Mixing spoon
- Large bowl or small foot tub

W hether you've been turning the soil in a garden bed or digging holes for your new apple trees, an hour or two of active gardening can be a physical challenge, especially to your feet. Before you start your day's gardening, brew the reward—the herbal decoction described here! Then, when your backyard chores are finished, pour yourself a tall glass of iced tea, find a comfortable chair, and pamper your aching toes and soles by soaking them in a small tub filled with the warm herbal solution of your choice.

Caution: If you tend toward skin allergies, by all means make an herbal decoction for a friend who doesn't, but don't use herbal decoctions yourself, as you may have an unexpected reaction.

Instructions

1 Place the herbs and water in the saucepan and bring the water to a boil.

2 Lower the heat, cover, and simmer for 30 minutes.

3 Line a sieve with two or three layers of cheesecloth, and place the sieve over a large bowl.

4 Pour the decoction into the lined sieve, and retain the strained liquid in the bowl.

5 Add the sea salt to the hot liquid, and stir to dissolve.

6 To make the foot-bath solution, pour hot water into a foot bath and then add one cup of the decoction.

7 Soak your feet in the bath for at least ten minutes. (Make sure you're resting in a comfortable chair as you do this.)

8 When you're finished, dry your feet well with a warm, fluffy towel.

Common Medicinal Plants

MEDICINAL PLANT	MEDICINAL PARTS	MEDICINAL USES
Basil *Ocimum basilicum*	leaves	tea taken internally to improve digestion and lower fever
Calendula *Calendula officinalis*	flowers	tincture applied externally to soothe skin problems; tea taken internally to soothe stomach inflammation
Chamomile *Chamaemelum nobile*	flowers	tea taken internally to aid digestion and improve appetite, and as a mild sedative
Lavender *Lavandula angustifolia*	flowers	essential oil used externally in baths as an aromatic aid for depression, fatigue, and headaches. Do not ingest essential oil.
Lemon balm *Melissa officinalis*	leaves	tea and tincture taken internally to relieve stress, insomnia, and indigestion
Mullein *Verbascum thapsus*	leaves and flowering tops	tea taken internally to relieve congestion
Parsley *Petroselinum crispum*	leaves	tea taken internally to relieve indigestion and congestion
Peppermint *Mentha piperita*	leaves	tea taken internally as an aid to digestion, to relieve headaches, and to reduce symptoms of stress. Do not give tea to infants.
Purple coneflower *Echinacea purpurea*	roots	tincture taken internally as an antiviral; should not be ingested by those with auto-immune illnesses or other progressive diseases
Rosemary *Rosmarinus officinalis*	leaves	tea or tincture taken internally to relieve headaches and as an anti-oxidant. Do not ingest essential oil.
Sage *Salvia officinalis*	leaves	tea taken internally to relieve symptoms of menopause, and as a gargle to alleviate sore throats. Do not use when nursing or running a fever.
Thyme *Thymus vulgaris*	leaves and flowering tops	tea taken internally to relieve sore throats, indigestion, headaches, and congestion
Yarrow *Achillea millefolium*	flowering tops	tea taken internally to aid digestion; tea applied externally to stop minor bleeding. (Use only on minor scratches.) May increase sensitivity to sunlight.

Gardening Basics

What's the difference between having a lovely garden and being a gardener? The first is certainly a worthy goal; a lush outdoor living space will provide you with pleasure for a lifetime. But the joy of having created that garden—with patience, love, and skill —is a joy unlike any other.

Becoming a true gardener is a gradual process. How will you know when you're no longer a beginner? When you grab a well-made trowel from the tool rack one day, and you're suddenly awed by how right it feels in your hand—by its balance and heft. When you can't sleep past dawn because the spring soil has finally dried out enough to cultivate. When you start hectoring your friends to save their wilted lettuce leaves and eggshells for your compost pile.

At first, you may not be aware of how quickly you're progressing toward a true love of gardening. But the day you find that setting out tender young seedlings, turning the rich earth in a garden bed, or puttering at your potting bench is no longer a chore, you've arrived. Before long, you may even find the sight, scent, and feel of dark, fertile loam as beautiful as any flower you grow in it.

Building a Potting Bench

Although this potting bench may never win prizes in the "elegant garden furniture" category, it's perfect for the backyard gardener—sturdy, functional, inexpensive, and unpretentious. You don't need to be an expert woodworker to construct it, either. In fact, this simple bench was designed for people who care more about puttering in their backyard gardens than developing expert woodworking skills.

MATERIALS & TOOLS

- Handsaw or circular saw
- Measuring tape
- Electric drill with ⅛" bit
- Hammer
- No. 2 Phillips-head screwdriver
- No. 6 decking screws, 2" and 1⅝"
- 12d (3¼") nails
- Primer and exterior paint (optional)
- Paintbrushes (optional)

TIPS

- Buying standard lumber that's the correct size can be confusing for beginning woodworkers because the numbers by which the board sizes are named (for example, 1 by 10, 1 by 12, and 2 by 4) don't represent the boards' actual sizes. A 2 by 4 (or 2 x 4) is approximately $1\frac{1}{2}$" thick and $3\frac{1}{2}$" wide. A 1 x 10 is about $\frac{3}{4}$" thick and $9\frac{1}{4}$" wide, and a 1 x 12 is about $\frac{3}{4}$" thick and $11\frac{1}{4}$" wide.

- The stringers (B), front piece (E), and spacers (F) in this project are all 2 x 4s that have been "ripped" (cut along their grain) to $2\frac{1}{2}$" in width. The easiest way to rip these boards is with a table saw, but if you don't have one, just substitute 2 x 4s cut to the correct lengths. Your finished potting bench may not look quite as graceful, but it will work just as well.

- The top and bottom shelves shown in the photo were actually made with $\frac{7}{8}$"-thick lumber. In the "Cutting List," however, they're replaced by $\frac{3}{4}$"-thick 1 x 10 and 1 x 12 lumber, which is sometimes easier to find.

- When the instructions call for drilling "pilot holes," use your drill and $\frac{1}{8}$" bit.

CUTTING LIST

CODE	DESCRIPTION	QTY.	MATERIAL
A	Legs	4	2 x 4 x 35"
B	Stringers	2	$1\frac{1}{2}$" x $2\frac{1}{2}$" x 20"
C	Side pieces	2	2 x 4 x 23"
D	Back piece	1	2 x 4 x 48"
E	Front piece	1	$1\frac{1}{2}$" x $2\frac{1}{2}$" x 48"
F	Spacers	2	$1\frac{1}{2}$" x $2\frac{1}{2}$" x 13"
G	Narrow bottom shelf	1	1 x 10 x 45"
H	Wide bottom shelf	1	1 x 12 x 45"
I	Top shelves	2	1 x 12 x 48"

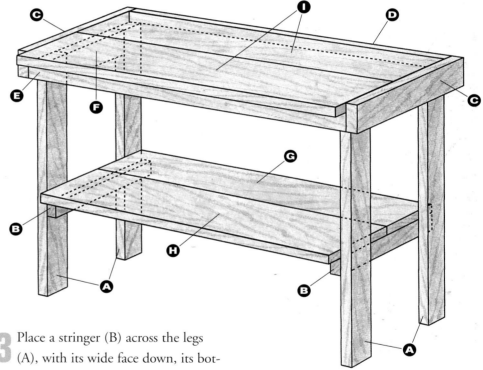

Instructions

1 Cut all the lumber to the lengths specified in the "Cutting List."

2 Place two legs (A) on a flat work surface, with their wide faces down and their outer edges 20" apart. Measure and mark a line across each leg (A), 12" up from its bottom end.

3 Place a stringer (B) across the legs (A), with its wide face down, its bottom edge at the 12" lines, and its ends flush with the outer edges of the legs (A). Fasten the stringer to the legs by drilling two pilot holes at each joint and then inserting 2" screws in the holes.

4 Repeat steps 2 through 3 to fasten the second stringer (B) to the remaining two legs (A).

5 At both ends of each side piece (C), measure and mark across the board's wide face, $\frac{3}{4}$" in from the end. Drill three evenly-spaced pilot holes along this line on one end of each side piece.

6 Position the side pieces (C) on edge, and insert the back piece (D), also on edge, between them so that the outer face of the back piece is flush with the end of each side piece. (Check to make sure that each side piece has three holes at this end.) Then secure the side pieces to the back piece by driving 12d nails through the pilot holes.

7 Position the front piece (E) so that its outer face is flush with the unsecured ends of the side pieces (C) and its lower edge is flush with the lower edges of the side pieces. (If you use a 2 x 4 for the front piece, position its upper edge ¾" below the upper edges of the side pieces. Its lower edge won't be flush with the lower edges of the side pieces.) To secure the side pieces to the front piece, first drill two evenly-spaced pilot holes through the ¾" line on each side piece. Then drive a 12d nail through each hole and into the front piece.

8 To attach a legs-and-stringer assembly (A and B) to the rectangular frame you have just made, first position the frame upright, with one side piece (C) flat on the work surface. Mark a straight line across the inner face of this side piece, ¾" down from its top edge.

9 Center a spacer (F), wide face down, on top of the side piece (C), so the spacer's top edge is flush with the ¾" line, and the lower edges of both parts are flush. (If the spacer is a 2 x 4, it won't rest flush at the bottom.)

10 Place the leg assembly (A and B) on top of the side piece (C). The ends of the legs should be flush with the top edge of the spacer (F) at the ¾" line, and the spacer should fill the space between the legs.

11 Drill three pilot holes through each leg (A) and into the side piece (C), and secure each leg to the side piece with three 2" screws.

12 Drill three evenly-spaced pilot holes through the spacer (F) and into the side piece (C), and secure the spacer with three 2" screws.

13 Repeat steps 8 through 12 to attach the other legs-and-stringer assembly (A and B) to the other end of the frame.

14 With the bench standing on its legs, position the narrow bottom shelf (G) across the back of the stringers (B); its outer edge should be flush with the ends of the stringers.

15 Drill two pilot holes through the narrow shelf (G) and into each stringer (B), about 1½" in from each edge of the shelf and ¾" in from its end. Secure the narrow shelf in place by driving 1⅝" screws through each pilot hole.

16 Position the wide bottom shelf (H) across the stringers (B) so that one edge is against the edge of the narrow bottom shelf (G), and the other edge overlaps the edges of the front legs by ½".

17 Drill two pilot holes at each end of the wide bottom shelf (H), about 1½" in from each long edge of the shelf and ¾" in from its end. Then fasten the shelf to each stringer (B) with two 1⅝" screws.

18 Repeat steps 14 through 17 to attach the top shelves (I) to the legs (A) and spacers (F). At the front of the potting bench, the top shelf will overlap the front piece (E) by 1".

19 If the bench will be exposed to the elements, be sure to apply a primer and a couple of coats of high-quality exterior paint.

Testing and Amending the Soil

Beneath every great gardener is a foot or two of healthy soil. If your plants could talk, most of them would ask for soil that drains well, is rich in organic matter, has a near-neutral pH, and contains plenty of available nutrients. Digging in the soil is one of the less glamorous aspects of gardening, but every hour you spend preparing and enriching your soil before you plant will pay off in the long run. Every attempt to ignore this fact and skimp on soil preparation will cause both you and your plants to suffer. Resisting that cheerful daisy gazing up from the sale table at the nursery may be difficult, but if you want your daisy to be happy and healthy three weeks later, you must first provide a fertile, friable home for the new plant.

SOIL TEXTURE

The ideal soil is made up of fine rock particles, organic matter, soil organisms, and open pore spaces that hold both water and air. The rock particles in soil are either sand, silt, or clay. Soil textures vary quite dramatically in different parts of the country, but they can also vary within your own yard. You need to know your soil's texture (or textures) in order to choose the plants best suited for the soil conditions and to amend the soil so you can grow a wider variety of plants.

Sandy soil feels gritty and is difficult to form into a ball. Since sandy soil doesn't hold water or nutrients well,

Clay soil, loam, sandy soil

acid or alkaline, the minerals in it bind together and become unavailable to your plants. Simple kits that test pH and fertility are available at most gardening centers. For a small fee, the Cooperative Extension Service in most states will provide a more detailed analysis of your soil.

Soil pH is measured on a scale of 1.0 to 14.0. Soil with a pH below 7.0 is acid (sour), while soil with a pH above 7.0 is alkaline (sweet). Most flowers prefer a pH of 6.0 to 7.0. If your garden's soil falls somewhere between 5.5 and 7.8, you can balance the pH level (up or down) simply by adding organic material. If your soil tests above or below this range, work with nature by focusing on plants that prefer the acid or alkaline conditions

your daisy will be thirsty and malnourished in it. Clay soil is slippery; when you squeeze it into a ball, it holds its shape without crumbling. This soil doesn't allow water to percolate adequately to plant roots, and it can be difficult to dig. Your daisy will struggle to send its roots out through this soil and might even drown.

To test the texture of your soil, add one cup of soil and one teaspoon of nonsudsing dishwasher detergent to a clean, one-quart glass jar. Fill the jar two-thirds full with water, place the lid on tightly, and shake it hard for two minutes; then set the jar on a level surface. After one minute, mark the outside of the jar to indicate where the soil has settled—this will be the sand layer. After two hours,

mark the new soil level—this is the silt layer. After two days, mark the final soil level—this is the clay layer. This will give you a visual "graph" of the percentage of each rock particle in your soil. Ideal soil (known as *loam*) is 40 percent silt, 40 percent sand, and 20 percent clay. If your soil has too much sand or clay, you can improve it by adding compost (see page 114) or other organic matter.

SOIL pH AND FERTILITY

You'll also want to test the pH level of your soil for acidity or alkalinity because these affect soil fertility. When soil is too

Most annuals, which tend to have shallow roots, will be happy with soil that's loosened to a depth of one foot. After removing any sod (and all but its smallest roots), insert your gardening spade one foot deep into the soil. Rock back and forth on the tool's handle to loosen the soil; then lift a spadeful of it, and flip the soil over. Repeat until the entire bed has been cultivated. Add any amendments on top of the loosened bed, and then work them into the soil with your spade or a gardening fork.

DOUBLE DIGGING

Your daisy (and other perennials) will thrive in double-dug soil. Once the sod is removed, double dig by excavating a trench across the bed that's one foot wide and one spade blade deep. Pile the soil from this trench onto a tarp or into a wheelbarrow. Next, use a gardening fork to loosen the soil in the trench's bottom, adding amendments such as compost as you do so. Dig another trench alongside the first one, but this time toss the topsoil onto the amended soil in the first trench. Loosen and amend the subsoil in the second trench. Repeat these steps to double dig the entire bed. Finally, place the reserved topsoil from the first trench on top of the subsoil in the last trench.

of your soil, or add amendments to adjust the pH. Dolomitic limestone will raise pH, and sulfur will lower it.

For strong roots and healthy leaves and flowers, your daisy (and most other plants) need nitrogen, phosphorus, and potassium from the soil, as well as a variety of trace elements. Compost, well-rotted cow manure, and leaf mold will provide most of the nutrition your plants require, while also improving soil texture. If you decide to add fertilizer, you'll need to choose between organic and inorganic types. Organic fertilizers are more environmentally safe, are less likely to burn plants, and don't pollute the environment. Inorganic fertilizers work more quickly and are easy to apply, but they leach out of the soil and into waterways, drive away earth-

worms, damage beneficial microorganisms, and can burn plants.

CULTIVATING THE SOIL

All the while that daisy's sunny-faced flowers are charming you above ground, its roots are laboring hard, tunneling through the soil in search of water and nutrients. Cultivation loosens the soil for roots and allows you to work in amendments. Make sure your soil is ready for digging; it should be slightly moist—not wet or dry—or you'll destroy its texture. Test soil readiness by picking up a fistful of soil and squeezing it into a ball. When you open your hand, the clump of soil should crumble. If it remains in a ball, the soil is too wet to dig; if it turns to dust, the soil is too dry.

Compost

Smart gardeners always have something rotting in their backyards. Something so valuable that it's called gardener's gold. Something made from ingredients that you may be in the habit of setting out on the curb for the trash collectors. That something, of course, is compost, and its effect on gardens is almost magical. Compost adds pore spaces to clay soil to loosen it and help it drain better. When added to sandy soil, compost helps the soil retain moisture and fertility. Compost is also chock-full of microorganisms that feed on organic matter and release nutrients to your plants.

COMPOST MATERIALS

You make compost by combining materials that are rich in nitrogen with materials that are rich in carbon. Common nitrogen sources (these tend to be moist and green) include fresh grass clippings and other green plant material, fruit and vegetable scraps, well-rotted manure, and coffee grounds. Carbon sources (typically brown and dry) include dry leaves, shredded bark or sticks, dry grass clippings, and hay or straw. The smaller you chop or shred these materials before adding them to the compost pile, the faster the microorganisms in the mixture will break them down. Do not add weeds, diseased plants, dairy products, meat or bones, or human or pet wastes to your compost pile.

MAKING COMPOST

Either the tortoise or the hare approach to composting will work. The tortoise approach is to pile mixed fresh green and dried brown yard wastes into a mound, add more yard waste as it be-comes available, and toss in a shovelful of fresh soil from time to time. During dry weather, aim the garden hose at your pile now and then. When your stack is three to four feet tall, start a new one. The completed pile will become usable compost, via benign neglect, in about a year and a half.

If you want compost and you want it now, you'll need to take the hare approach by creating optimum compost-pile conditions: an internal temperature of 140°F to 160°F (60°C to 71°C), adequate moisture, and good air circulation. Rotating composters, which are spun in order to aerate their contents thoroughly, can produce finished compost in only three or four weeks.

If neither the hare nor the tortoise route appeals to you, try a middle-of-the-road approach by composting in a low-tech plastic compost bin or in a simple cylinder of hardware cloth. Chopping materials finely, keeping the pile as moist as a damp sponge, and turning the pile every two to four weeks will all speed up the process.

USING COMPOST

Finished compost is dark brown, crumbles easily, and has a rich, earthy aroma. Work compost into the soil as an amendment during cultivation, or scatter it around plants as a top dressing. Compost tea (water in which compost has been steeped for several days) makes an excellent liquid fertilizer.

Putting in Plants

You've made your soil all fertile and fluffy. You've purchased your containers of plants, and you're ready to tuck them into their new homes. Take a few extra precautions to get them off to a good start, and they'll thank you with robust foliage and abundant flowers.

GETTING STARTED

The move from container to soil is stressful for plants, so pamper them. To guard against wilting, give the plants a long drink while they're still in their pots and plant on an overcast day or in the early evening. Remove most flowers and pinch leggy growth from annuals before you plant them to encourage strong root growth and a summer's worth of blooms.

Before you start digging holes for the plants, set them in their containers on your garden bed, spaced according to label instructions. (If labels are missing or instructions aren't provided, check a plant encyclopedia for proper planting distances.) Plants look best grouped in odd numbers, so set them out in clusters of three, five, or seven.

PLANTING

Dig a hole almost twice as wide and deep as the plant's container. Refill the hole with amended soil (see page 111) until the hole is as deep as the height

of the container. Then carefully remove the plant by turning its pot upside down and tapping the bottom. (Don't tug on the plant's stem; if you can't get the plant and soil ball out easily, carefully cut the container apart.)

Gently loosen any tangled roots and adjust the hole if necessary so the roots fit without breaking or bending. Place the plant in the hole, making sure it sits at the same soil level as it did in its container.

Refill the hole around the plant with the excavated soil, press the top of the soil gently to remove any air pockets, and then water the plant thoroughly. (As always, a gentle soaking will allow

the water to be absorbed down near the plant's roots.) When all your plants are in, spread a two- to four-inch layer of mulch over the bed, leaving a two-inch diameter circle around each plant's stem to prevent rot.

If your new transplants are in an especially sunny spot, you may want to rig up some temporary shade to help them through the first few days of the move. Water all plants well until they're established. The stress of transplanting makes your plants less able to tolerate lack of water, insect damage, and diseases, so check on them often for the first couple of weeks they are in their new homes.

Mulch

Of course you don't really *want* to mulch your garden. Napping in the dappled shade of your pergola or splashing in the sprinkler while you water the lawn would be much more pleasant ways to pass an afternoon. But mulching correctly will save you from many a day of gardening chores. A blanket of mulch helps retain moisture in your soil, while regulating soil temperatures and suppressing weeds. Mulch works to prevent soil-

borne diseases from reaching your plants and prevents dirt from splashing up onto flowers and leaves. It also insulates against soil shifts from repeated freezes and thaws in winter, and eventually decomposes to add organic matter to the soil. On top of all that, mulch is to gorgeous gardens as makeup is to Hollywood starlets—it makes them look terrific.

MULCH MATERIALS

Pine needles, straw, leaf mold, dried grass clippings, compost, shredded bark, and bark nuggets are all organic mulches. Sand and gravel are some-

times used as mulch around plants that thrive in hot, dry conditions. Inorganic mulches such as black plastic and landscape fabric suppress weeds, but they also prevent perennials from spreading, and they don't add organic matter to the soil.

USING MULCH

Mulch perennials when most of the new growth has sprouted, after the soil has warmed up in spring and you've removed all weeds. When starting plants from seed, apply mulch only after you've thinned the seedlings and the remaining ones have several sets of

leaves. Transplants can usually be mulched as soon as they're set out. A two- to four-inch-thick layer of mulch is generally recommended. To prevent rot, push the mulch back a couple of inches from plant stems or tree trunks.

Winter mulches are also useful. They are not meant to keep plants warm but to insulate the soil from sudden freezes and thaws, which can push plants out of the ground and kill them. Airy materials, such as straw, hay, and pine boughs, serve especially well as winter mulches. If you live in an area of heavy snows, you're in luck: Snow is nature's ideal winter mulch.

Garden Tools

Ask anyone who has gardened for a while, and he or she will tell you the same thing: Buy the highest quality tools you can afford. You'll save money in the long run, and you'll have more fun gardening right from the start. Settle for a flimsy hand trowel, and you'll have to stop to bend its blade back into position each time you dig into solid ground. Then, just when you've set aside an afternoon for leisurely gardening, the handle of that trowel is bound to snap off, and you'll have to spend your afternoon buying another one instead. (Either that, or ruin one of your large kitchen spoons!)

SELECTING TOOLS

This doesn't mean you have to order designer tools from glossy catalogs, but do look for tools with blades made from forged or tempered high-carbon steel (or stainless steel) and handles made from straight-grained ash or hickory (or high-strength fiberglass). The most vulnerable part of a tool is the blade extension—where the blade and handle meet. It should be strong and surround the handle completely. If your budget is limited, purchase just a few of the most essential tools (a spade, a hand trowel, and a hose are good choices). Also, try shopping at yard sales and flea markets for high-quality, used tools at affordable prices.

Make sure the tools you choose are the size and weight that feels most comfortable to you.

MAINTAINING TOOLS

Extend the life and efficiency of your tools by keeping them clean and sharp. Most tools can be hosed down as long as you dry them thoroughly afterward. Wipe the blades with an oily rag after each use. To prevent splinters, sand wooden handles lightly, and rub these handles with linseed oil at least once a year to preserve them.

Also, keep your tools sharp; they'll perform more efficiently and make cleaner cuts, which in turn will keep plants healthier.

Store your tools in an accessible, dry spot. Hanging tools on a wall is usually the easiest way to organize your storage space so that you can locate each tool quickly. Get in the habit of returning each tool to the same spot; you'll spend less time looking for those pruning shears you left under the lilac bush and more time enjoying your garden.

Building a Garden Tool Shelf

Remember the last time you found a rusted trowel half-buried in a garden bed? Or discovered your favorite clippers hiding beneath a pile of mulch? This project—the perfect home for wayward gardening tools and supplies—was designed for you. Just set aside a free afternoon, gather some inexpensive materials and a few basic tools, and follow the simple instructions.

MATERIALS & TOOLS

- Handsaw or circular saw
- Pencil
- Tape measure
- Straightedge
- Electric drill with ⅛" bit and 1" spade bit
- Wood glue
- No. 2 Phillips-head screwdriver
- No. 6 decking screws, 1¼" and 1⅝"
- Sandpaper
- Paint or finish (optional)

TIPS

- When you purchase the front trim stock, ask for ¾" "S4S" (surface four square) stock or any narrow molding.
- Rectangular 4' x 8' sheets of lattice are available at many home-improvement centers. Have the sheet cut to size for you there.
- Use your drill and ⅛" bit to drill pilot holes at every screw location. These holes will make inserting the screws much easier. Unless the instructions tell you otherwise, locate the holes ⅜" in from each board's edge.

Instructions

1 Cut all the parts except for the lattice (see "Tips") to the lengths specified in the "Cutting List."

2 To mark holes in each side panel (B) for the dowel rod (C), measure and mark a point 2¾" up from one end of the side panel and 2¾" in from either of its edges.

3 Using a drill and 1" spade bit, carefully bore a hole at each mark, but stop drilling as soon as the point of the bit begins to exit from the opposite face of the board. (The dowel will fit into the 1"-wide portion of the hole, and the narrow opening left by the point of the bit will serve as a pilot hole.)

4 Place the upper shelf (A) on the tops of the side panels (B). Drill a row of three evenly-spaced pilot holes through the upper shelf and into each end of a side panel.

5 Apply wood glue to the ends of the dowel rod (C), and insert the ends of the rod into the holes in the side panels (B). Then fasten the upper shelf (A) to the side panels (B) with three 1⅝" screws through each joint.

6 After drilling a pilot hole, secure the dowel rod (C) by inserting a 1¼" screw through each side panel (B) and into the rod.

7 Measure 24¾" down from the top face of the upper shelf (A), and mark a line across the outer face of each side panel (B).

8 Along each of the 24¾" lines on the side panels (B), drill three evenly-spaced pilot holes. To complete the tool rack frame, fasten the lower shelf (D) to the sides (B) by inserting 1⅝" screws through the pilot holes.

9 Check the lattice (E) for fit by placing it into the opening formed by the sides (B) and the shelves (A and D). Trim the lattice if necessary, and set it aside.

CUTTING LIST

CODE	DESCRIPTION	QTY.	MATERIAL
A	Upper shelf	1	1 x 6 x 49"
B	Side panel	2	1 x 6 x 30"
C	Dowel rod	1	1" diameter x 48¾"
D	Lower shelf	1	1 x 6 x 47½"
E	⅜" lattice	1	23⅝" x 47½"
F	Long rear trim pieces	2	1 x 2 x 49"
G	Short rear trim pieces	2	1 x 2 x 22⅛"
H	Long front trim pieces	2	¾" x ¾" x 47½"
I	Short front trim pieces	2	¾" x ¾" x 22⅛"

10 Using four evenly-spaced 1¼" screws, attach one of the two long rear trim pieces (F) to the back of the upper shelf (A), with its wide face down and its upper edge flush with the upper face of the shelf. Attach the other long rear trim piece in the same fashion, positioning its bottom edge flush with the bottom face of the lower shelf (D).

11 Position and secure the two short rear trim pieces (G) in the same fashion, using three 1¼" screws on each piece. Make sure the outer

edge of each short trim piece is flush with the outer face of a side (B).

12 Place the assembled frame, trim side down, on a flat work surface. Then position the lattice in the assembly.

13 To secure the lattice in place, position the long and short front trim pieces (H and I) against the lattice, as shown in the illustration. Attach the long trim pieces with four evenly-spaced 1¼" screws driven into the top face of the lower shelf, and the short trim pieces with three evenly-spaced 1¼" screws driven into the inner faces of the sides.

14 Using sandpaper, round over and smooth all the edges.

15 Paint or finish the tool rack as desired.

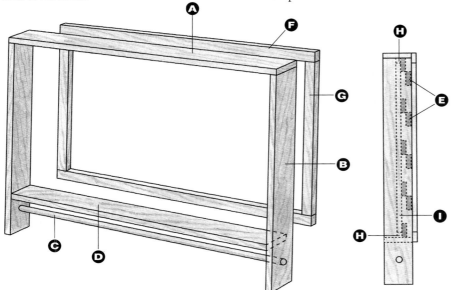

Good Bugs, Bad Bugs

When a slimy slug munches its way through your prized hosta leaves, leaving lacy green doilies behind, you may be tempted to adopt the motto that the only good bug is a dead bug. The truth is, it's a bug-eat-bug world in your garden, and some of those bugs are on your side. Learning which insects nibble leaves and which insects eat the leaf nibblers will help you work with nature, rather than against it, to keep your garden healthy.

THE BAD GUYS

The thugs in your yard will usually leave clues behind. Slugs and snails like to dine while you're sleeping or on cool, cloudy days. Trailing slime to and from the scene of the crime, they consume seedlings and sometimes entire leaves or chomp ragged holes in

Praying mantis

Garden slug

the foliage of low growing plants. The more precise Japanese beetle chews round or oblong holes in flowers and leaves (unless it decides to eat the whole leaf; then it will devour all but a skeleton of leaf veins). Aphids—tiny, pear-shaped insects—leave distorted, curled, and sticky leaves in their wake. The larvae of leafminers feed between the upper and lower surfaces of leaves. Maze-like tunnels, blotches, and blisters are all evidence that they've been feasting on your foliage.

THE GOOD GUYS

It's important to remember that at the same time aphids are sucking on your tulip stems, another insect is out there, ready to sup on the aphids.

Those cute, polka-dotted ladybugs (also called lady beetles or lady birds) strike terror in the hearts of many garden pests who know there's nothing ladylike about the beetles' appetite for bad bugs. Parasitic wasps and tachinid flies lay their eggs in caterpillars and other bugs so their larvae hatch inside their first meal. A delicate spider web, bejewelled with morning dew, is actually a deadly snare set to entangle a bug that will become the arachnid's lunch. The praying mantis is not worshipping; its lethal forelimbs are poised for attack.

Encourage beneficial insects to take up residence in your yard by providing a few luxuries for them. Most require water (a one- to two-inch-deep container with a small stone to serve as a raft works well). Plants that attract beneficial insects include dill, coriander, fennel, lavender, black-eyed Susan, and Queen-Anne's-lace.

Most important, unless your garden is suffering from a downright plague of destructive insects, don't panic and reach for the poisons as soon as you see insect damage. Pesticides kill not only the bad guys but also your allies in the battle of the bugs. Most plants recover from insect attacks, and a few holes in your zinnia leaves won't matter in the long run.

THE CONVERTS

Finally, we have the bad guys who reform. Before resorting to chemical sprays, remind yourself that those caterpillars you are cursing now may metamorphize into lovely butterflies. That tomato hornworm devouring vegetables will soon be a sphinx moth pollinating night-blooming flowers. Read a good book on garden insects to learn to identify friend from foe. Then welcome beneficial insects into your yard while using more selective (and environmentally friendly) ways to give the bad guys the boot.

Tomato hornworm

REPELLING THE HORDES

Don't despair if the leaf-munching hordes in your garden outnumber the beneficial bugs. An entire arsenal of home remedies exists to help you snuff out those bad bugs—or at least send them scurrying. Following are a few examples:

- Place several grapefruit rinds upside down in your garden (melon rinds or cabbage leaves will also work); slugs will be attracted to their protection and shade. Check the rinds early in the morning and destroy the slumbering slugs and any other insects that have availed themselves of your hospitality.
- Study up on companion planting. Many believe that planting garlic near roses will repel Japanese beetles. Both marigolds and nasturtiums are said to send a variety of garden pests packing.
- Make a toad abode out of an overturned clay pot, with a hole broken out for a door. Insects make up 90 percent of a toad's diet.
- For an effective spray, steep a dozen minced garlic cloves in one pint of mineral oil for 24 hours. Strain out the garlic, and add one teaspoon of liquid dish soap. Remember when using this spray that it can also harm beneficial insects.
- Use a hand-held vacuum to suck beetles and other insects off your plants. Just remember to empty the pests from your bug-buster and destroy them.

Water-Thrifty Gardening

Daylilies and purple coneflowers

Let's face it: A garden can be demanding. Without a certain amount of tender loving care, plants will fold in the face of the elements. After a particularly ruthless day of sun, you'll probably have to unwind the hose and soak those garden beds until each drooping flower looks happy again. But garden watering should be more than a matter of damage control. To keep plants thriving and not just surviving, you'll need to devise a regular watering program—one that satiates both your backyard soil and the vegetation it supports, while conserving water and time.

XERISCAPING

As municipal water supplies decline and unpredictable weather patterns increase, it's more important than ever to work with, rather than against, your yard's ecosystem. One way to do this is by learning the art of xeriscaping. Derived from the Greek word *xeros*, which means dry, xeriscaping is actually a method of landscaping that conserves water. Plan your garden with xeriscaping in mind, and you'll save yourself hours of garden maintenance down the road.

First, as you design your backyard, group together plants with common watering needs. There's an obvious

logic to segregating roses and rhododendrons from daylilies and coneflowers: The water required to keep the former healthy would be wasted on the latter. You can grow thirsty plants such as roses, but do so in an area that you've designated as water-intensive—preferably close to your water source.

Selecting native plants and wildflowers that have naturalized in your area is another wise way to keep garden maintenance to a minimum. After all, if a plant thrives naturally in your region, without the benefit of water from a hose or sprinkler, chances are it will flourish in your backyard with very little attention. Coreopsis, Stokes' aster, and blue flax are just a few of the many drought-resistant wildflowers to consider. Native-plant societies and local arboretums can suggest many more plants for your region. You may be surprised to learn

that some species of the prickly pear cactus are not only water-thrifty, but are also natives as far north as Canada.

Another vital aspect of xeriscaping is attention to soil quality. Keeping your soil well-drained and moisture retentive allows your garden to do more with the water it's given. A layer of mulch such as leaf mold will help improve soil quality as it decomposes, reduce weed growth by smothering weed seedlings, minimize competition among plants for water, and reduce evaporation by cooling the soil beneath it.

IRRIGATION

After planting your garden with an eye to water conservation, the next step is to design a watering program. The rule of thumb is that plants need an inch of water per week. This rule can be difficult to apply, however, given the countless variables involved: how much sun each plant gets, the soil composition in its bed, and the vagaries of the weather.

The real trick to keep in mind is that when you water (typically about once a week for most perennials), always water deeply. If you continually supply water only to the top few inches of soil, your plants will form shallow root systems. This is harmful since the top few inches of soil heat up and dry out more quickly than the soil farther down. Instead, soak the soil slowly until it is moist to a depth of 12 inches. This will encourage

Prickly pear cactus

roots to penetrate deep into the soil. Deeply rooted plants can tap into the soil's moisture reserves during dry spells, and they are also well-anchored and able to reach soil nutrients.

The most efficient, low-maintenance tools for deep watering are soaker hoses and drip systems. A soaker hose generally consists of a single length of foam, vinyl, or rubber tubing, with holes along its length. Water seeps out to soak a two- to three-foot-wide band around the hose. To implement this type of irrigation, simply snake the hose through your garden and turn on the tap.

Drip systems, which consist of multiple hose components, are slightly more complex than soaker hoses, but are much more efficient. Why? Because you can assemble the hose

components so that their drip points are right where you want them to be— over the root zones of specific plants. Unlike a soaker hose, which releases water along its entire length, a drip system can be tailored to the actual layout of your garden.

And one final water-conservation tip: No matter how thirsty your plants look at midday, resist the temptation to water them right away. Fifty to seventy-five percent of any water you provide during the hottest part of the day will evaporate. Avoid watering in the evening, too; you'll just be providing an open invitation to slugs and diseases. Wait until morning to give your plants a drink. Stems will rise, blossoms will perk, and leaves will spread. Your plants will thank you.

Hardiness-Zone Map

A plant's winter hardiness is critical in deciding whether it is suitable for your garden. The map below divides the United States and Canada into 11 climatic zones based on average minimum temperatures, as compiled by the U.S. Department of Agriculture. Find your zone and check the zone information in the garden plans to help you choose the plants most likely to flourish in your climate.

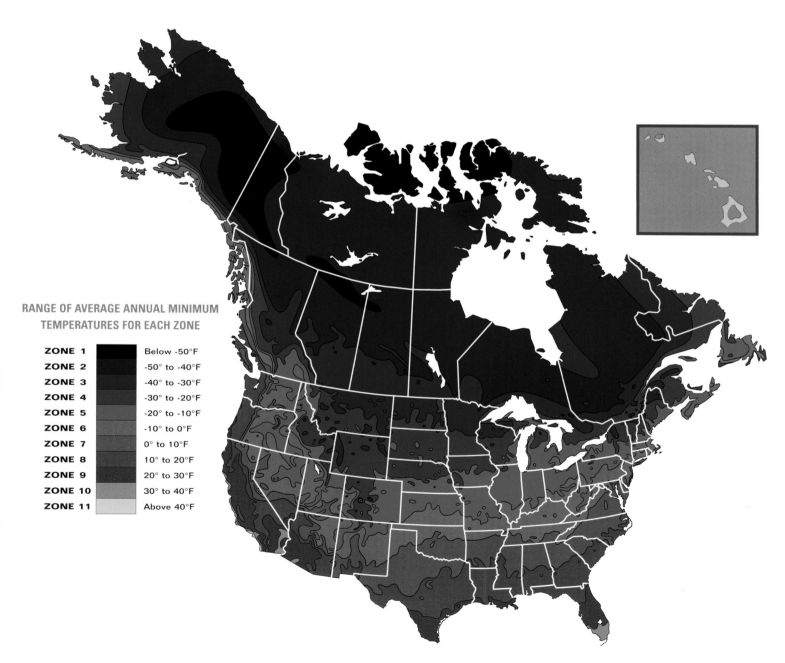

RANGE OF AVERAGE ANNUAL MINIMUM TEMPERATURES FOR EACH ZONE

ZONE 1	Below -50°F
ZONE 2	-50° to -40°F
ZONE 3	-40° to -30°F
ZONE 4	-30° to -20°F
ZONE 5	-20° to -10°F
ZONE 6	-10° to 0°F
ZONE 7	0° to 10°F
ZONE 8	10° to 20°F
ZONE 9	20° to 30°F
ZONE 10	30° to 40°F
ZONE 11	Above 40°F

Acknowledgments

PHOTOGRAPHY

For his amazing skill, his humor, and his support, special thanks to photographer Evan Bracken (Light Reflections, Hendersonville, NC), who took most of the photographs in this book. All photographs not otherwise credited are by Mr. Bracken.

For all his hard work and for his magical touch, heartfelt thanks to photo stylist Skip Wade.

Thanks also to photographer and praying mantis wrangler Richard Hasselberg (Black Mountain, NC), whose photos appear on pages 12, 45 (center), 46, 48, 49, 50, 51 (center), 70, 74, 91 (top, right), 98 (left), 99 (bottom), 100, 112 (top), 120 (top), and 121 (bottom).

We are deeply grateful to the following for their generous photographic contributions: Mary Brittain (The Cottage Gardener Heirloom Plant Nursery, Ontario, Canada), pages 92 and 93; Gary Chandler (McKenzie, TN), pages 77 (top), 82, 83 (top), 84, and 85 (top); Robin Dreyer (Celo, NC), page 122 (top); Christine Dombrowski (Dallas Horticultural Center, Dallas, TX), pages 96 (top) and 97; Clyde S. Gorsuch (Dept. of Entomology, Clemson University, Clemson, SC), page 121 (top); Monrovia (Azusa, CA, 1-888-PLANT IT), pages 22 (bottom) and 83; Steven J. Prchal (Sonoran Anthropod Studies Institute, Tucson, AZ), page 75; Hunter Stubbs (horticulturalist and photographer, Richmond Hill Inn, Asheville, NC), pages 10 (right), 16, and 30.

LOCATIONS

Very special thanks to Dr. Peter and Jasmine Gentling for sharing their extensive horticultural knowledge and allowing us to photograph their exquisite gardens.

Many thanks to the following North Carolina residents for permission to take photographs of their gardens. Their generosity, patience, and encouragement made this book possible: Jan and Simon Braun (Asheville); Cindy Causby and Dave Campbell (Asheville); Diane Rodgers Claybrook (Asheville); John Cram (Kenilworth Gardens, Asheville); Eve Davis (Hawk and Ivy Bed & Breakfast, Barnardsville); Susan Fennelly and Ken Minnich (Asheville); Hedy Fischer and Randy Shull (Asheville); Rick and Gwenn Ford (Asheville); Robert and Jacqueline Glasgow (Beaufort House Victorian Bed & Breakfast, Asheville); Dr. Stewart and Debbie Harley (Biltmore Forest); Stephanie Harris (Asheville); Carol Hire (Asheville); Steven and Martha Howard (Asheville); Randall and Mary Johnson (Asheville); Chris and Melonie Knorr (Asheville); Karl and Beth Lail (Asheville); Peter Loewer (Asheville); Marla Murphy (Gourmet Gardens Herb Farm, Weaverville); Richmond Hill Inn (Asheville); Bonnie Sheldon (Asheville); Colleen Sikes (Asheville); C.B. Squires (Herb Mountain L.P., Weaverville); Taylor and Webb (Asheville); Linda Tuuri (Asheville); University of North Carolina at Asheville Botanical Gardens (Asheville); Dr. Peter and Cathy Wallenborn (Asheville); Kenneth and Claudia Wienke (Asheville); Patricia and Gary Wiles (Cumberland Falls Bed & Breakfast, Asheville); Dr. John Wilson (Black Mountain); Lassie York Woody (Asheville); Lisa and Rice Yordy (The Lion & the Rose Bed & Breakfast, Asheville)

PROJECT DESIGN

Our thanks to the following project designers: Kevin Barnes (Asheville, NC): rustic bench, page 42; Robin Clark (Asheville, NC): trellis planter, page 32; potting bench, page 108; tool shelf, page 118; Amy Cook (Asheville, NC): garden journal, page 80.

RESEARCH AND WRITING

For their research and writing skills, we are indebted to: Trent Bouts (Asheville, NC); Amy Cook (Asheville, NC); Holly Clark (Leicester, NC); Naomi Friedman (Asheville, NC); Clare Hanrahan (Asheville, NC); Megan Kirby (Asheville, NC).

Thanks also to our superb indexer, Jackie Flenner (Asheville, NC).

ADVICE AND INFORMATION

For his horticultural advice, magnificent ponds and waterfalls, and help with location scouting, we thank Steve Haun (Tanbark Landscape Company, Inc., Asheville, NC).

For the information accompanying the miniature orchard plan on page 59, we thank Hunter and Donna Carleton (Bear Creek Nursery, Northport, WA, 99157).

For research assistance, thanks to Malaprops Bookstore (Asheville, NC).

Bibliography

Adams, George. *Birdscaping Your Garden.* Emmaus, Pa.: Rodale Press, 1994.

Appleton, Bonnie Lee, and Alfred F. Scheidler. *Rodale's Successful Organic Gardening: Trees, Shrubs, and Vines.* Emmaus, Pa.: Rodale Press, 1993.

Ausubel, Kenny. *Seeds of Change: The Living Treasure.* San Francisco: HarperSanFrancisco, 1994.

Ball, Jeff, and Liz Ball. *Yardening.* New York: Macmillan Publishing Company, 1991.

Barash, Cathy Wilkinson. *Evening Gardens: Planning & Planting a Landscape to Dazzle the Senses after Sundown.* Shelburne, Vt.: Chapters Publishing, Ltd., 1993.

Barash, Cathy Wilkinson, and Jim Wilson. *The Cultivated Gardener.* New York: Simon and Schuster, 1996.

Bender, Steve and Felder Rushing. *Passalong Plants.* Chapel Hill, N.C.: The University of North Carolina Press, 1993.

The Big Book of Flower Gardening. Alexandria, Va.: Time-Life Books, 1996.

Blose, Norma, and Dawn Cusick. *Herb Drying Handbook.* New York: Sterling Publishing Co., Inc., 1993.

Bradley, Fern Marshall, ed. *Gardening with Perennials.* Emmaus, Pa.: Rodale Press, 1996.

Cathey, H. Marc, with Linda Bellamy. *Heat-Zone Gardening.* Alexandria, Va.: Time-Life Books, 1998.

Cave, Janet, ed. *Perennials.* Alexandria, Va.: Time-Life Books, 1995.

Clarke, Ethne. *Water Features for Small Gardens.* New York: Sterling Publishing Co., Inc., 1998.

Cook, Ferris. *The Garden Trellis: Designs to Build and Vines to Cultivate.* New York: Artisan, 1996.

Cox, Jeff. *Decorating Your Garden.* New York: Abbeville Press, 1999.

Creasy, Rosalind. *Cooking from the Garden.* San Francisco: Sierra Club Books, 1988.

Dannenmaier, Molly. *A Child's Garden: Enchanting Outdoor Spaces for Children and Parents.* New York: Simon & Schuster, 1998.

Erler, Catriona Tudor. *Garden Rooms: Creating and Decorating Garden Spaces.* Alexandria, Va.: Time-Life Books, 1999.

Evans, Hazel. *The Patio Garden.* New York: Viking and Penguin Books, 1986.

Lacy, Allen. *The Inviting Garden: Gardening for the Senses, Mind, and Spirit.* New York: Henry Holt and Company, 1998.

LaLiberte, Katherine, and Ben Watson. *Gardener's Supply Company Passport to Gardening: A Sourcebook for the 21st-Century Gardener.* White River Junction, Vt.: Chelsea Green Publishing Company, 1997.

Loewer, Peter. *The Evening Garden.* New York: Macmillan Publishing Company, 1993.

Michalak, Patricia S. *Controlling Pests and Diseases.* Emmaus, Pa.: Rodale Press, 1994.

Nash, Helen. *Low-Maintenance Water Gardens.* New York: Sterling Publishing Co., Inc., 1996.

Ody, Penelope. *The Complete Medicinal Herbal.* New York: DK Publishing, 1993.

Reed, David. *The Art and Craft of Stonescaping.* Asheville, N.C.: Lark Books, 1998.

Rodale's No-Fail Flower Gardens. Emmaus, Pa.: Rodale Press, 1994.

Rosenstein, Mark. *In Praise of Apples: A Harvest of History, Horticulture & Recipes.* Asheville, N.C.: Lark Books, 1996.

Sombke, Laurence. *Beautiful Easy Flower Gardens.* Emmaus, Pa.: Rodale Press, 1995.

Taylor, Patricia, A. *Step-by-Step Shade Gardens.* Des Moines, Iowa: Better Homes and Gardens® Books, 1995.

Time-Life How-To Garden Designs: Simple Steps to Beautiful Flower Gardens. Alexandria, Va.: Time-Life Books, 1997.

Tufts, Craig, and Peter Loewer. *Gardening for Wildlife.* Emmaus, Pa.: Rodale Press, 1995.

von Trapp, Sara Jane. *Landscaping from the Ground Up.* Newton, Conn.: The Tauton Press, 1997.

Yard & Garden Projects: Easy, Step-by-Step Plans and Designs for Beautiful Outdoor Spaces. Alexandria, Va.: Time-Life Books, 1998.

Metric Conversions

Length

Inches	CM		
1/8	0.3	19	48.3
1/4	0.6	20	50.8
3/8	1.0	21	53.3
1/2	1.3	22	55.9
5/8	1.6	23	58.4
3/4	1.9	24	61.0
7/8	2.2	25	63.5
1	2.5	26	66.0
1 1/4	3.2	27	68.6
1 1/2	3.8	28	71.1
1 3/4	4.4	29	73.7
2	5.1	30	76.2
2 1/2	6.4	31	78.7
3	7.6	32	81.3
3 1/2	8.9	33	83.8
4	10.2	34	86.4
4 1/2	11.4	35	88.9
5	12.7	36	91.4
6	15.2	37	94.0
7	17.8	38	96.5
8	20.3	39	99.1
9	22.9	40	101.6
10	25.4	41	104.1
11	27.9	42	106.7
12	30.5	43	109.2
13	33.0	44	111.8
14	35.6	45	114.3
15	38.1	46	116.8
16	40.6	47	119.4
17	43.2	48	121.9
18	45.7	49	124.5
		50	127.0

Volume

1 fluid ounce = 29.6 ml
1 pint = 473 ml
1 quart = 946 ml
1 gallon (128 fl. oz.) = 3.785 liters

liters x .2642 = gallons
liters x 2.11 = pints
liters x 33.8 = fluid ounces
gallons x 3.785 = liters
gallons x .1337 = cubic feet
cubic feet x 7.481 = gallons
cubic feet x 28.32 = liters

Weight

0.035 ounces = 1 gram
1 ounce = 28.35 grams
1 pound = 453.6 grams

grams x .0353 = ounces
grams x .0022 = pounds
ounces x 28.35 = grams
pounds x 453.6 = grams
tons (short) x 907.2 = kilograms
tons (metric) x 2205 = pounds
kilograms x .0011 = tons (short)
pounds x .00045 = tons (metric)

Index